+15 —
SB1757

THE CRESSET LIBRARY

GENERAL EDITOR: JOHN HAYWARD

A MEMOIR OF THOMAS BEWICK

THOMAS BEWICK

1753–1828

A MEMOIR
OF
THOMAS BEWICK

written by himself

Edited and with an introduction by
MONTAGUE WEEKLEY

WITH WOOD ENGRAVINGS BY
THOMAS BEWICK

LONDON
THE CRESSET PRESS
1961

Printed in Great Britain by the Shenval Press
London, Hertford and Harlow

PREFACE

The abridged text here presented derives from a collation of the fullest previous edition of the *Memoir*, edited by Austin Dobson and published in 1887, with Bewick's autograph manuscript in the British Museum. Much of the memoir consists of fascinating recollections; it is, alas, also burdened with prolix discursions into religion and ethics, devoid of biographical interest. The Introduction which follows dwells at greater length on the problems confronting an editor of Bewick's *Memoir*, which, in so far as it tells the story of his life, is among the most absorbing autobiographies ever penned.

The Publishers tender their grateful thanks to the Oxford University Press for the loan of the block made from Miss Joan Hassall's wood-engraved portrait of Bewick, which appeared on the title-page of the Editor's *Thomas Bewick* (1953). They are further indebted to the Oxford University Press for the generous loan of eleven blocks for illustrations to that work. The blocks of the Magpie and of the tailpiece depicting Bewick riding in a coach were kindly lent by Penguin Books. Mr Sydney Roscoe, Bewick's bibliographer and pre-eminent among Bewick collectors, has been so kind as to furnish precise references to Bewick's books for the figures of beasts and birds, and for the tailpieces reproduced in this edition of the *Memoir*.

The Editor's footnotes are distinguished from Bewick's by being enclosed in square brackets.

CONTENTS

x

ILLUSTRATIONS

Frontispiece: Wood-engraving by Joan Hassall from the marble bust of Bewick (Literary and Philosophical Society of Newcastle) by Edward Hodges Baily, R.A. (1788–1867). Note gravers, leather sandbag on which to turn the block while engraving, eye-glass, and water globe through which to concentrate lamplight on the work.

From Jane Bewick's interleaved copy of the Birds (1821), where she inked over notes, relating to the figures and tailpieces, which her father had pencilled. Library, Victoria and Albert Museum, London.

N.B. Bewick did not attach descriptions to his tailpieces. The titles printed in italic refer to the books where they first appeared.

INTRODUCTION

To what does Thomas Bewick (1753–1828) owe his fame? He stands pre-eminent among wood-engravers, he ranks with the greatest illustrators, and his autobiography is unique as the account of an artist-tradesman's life in the England of George III. Bewick, the artist-tradesman, was in business at Newcastle-upon-Tyne as a miscellaneous engraver, with a workshop in St Nicholas's Churchyard.

The exact date of Bewick's birth is uncertain. In a letter giving a summary of his career, Bewick wrote that he was born on August 10, 1753, whereas a commemorative tablet in Ovingham Church has August 12. The account of his childhood in the Tyne valley is perhaps the most attractive part of his autobiography. John Bewick, his father, had the modest farm of Cherryburn, resting on the slope above the Tyne's steeper south bank which leads up to Mickley, where he also rented a small colliery. Part of Cherryburn Cottage, Bewick's birthplace, survives as a whitewashed outhouse to a larger dwelling built early in the nineteenth century. Mickley is still a colliery village. Cherryburn belongs to the hamlet of Eltringham which is part of the ancient parish of Ovingham on the river's opposite (north) bank, some twelve miles from Newcastle.

Bewick wonderfully describes the scenery of the Tyne valley, then wilder and more heavily wooded, where he enjoyed a rapturous boyhood. Exceptional powers of observation and the stimulus of such early surroundings made him a keen naturalist, whose recollections dwell much on his enthusiasm for bird watching and the life of field and farm. The *Memoir* scarcely hints at the wealth of history amid which Bewick grew up although the stretch of river from Newcastle to Hexham is rich in Roman remains, castles, and ancient churches belonging to Northumbria's Christian culture inspired by Aidan and Cuthbert. Northumbrian castles and churches do, however, appear in some of Bewick's tailpieces, the most memorable aspect of his mature work as a wood-engraver for book illustration.

Ovingham was always the centre of Bewick's Tyne valley. He lies buried beneath the church's Saxon tower, recognizable in some of his wood-engravings, which presides over a village where, more than two hundred years after his birth, stand the vicarage in which he had most of his schooling, and farm buildings typical of those depicted in Bewick tailpieces. Ovingham's seventeenth-century parsonage, retaining a fifteenth-century window from an earlier building, seems to be little altered since the days of Bewick's 'revered preceptor', the Rev Christopher Gregson. Like Oliver Goldsmith's parson father, Gregson supplemented a meagre clerical stipend by farming, but he also kept a school. A large upper room, with windows overlooking the Tyne, is said to have been the schoolroom.

The *Memoir* dwells much on Bewick's passion for drawing, evident at a very early age, which led to his apprenticeship to Ralph Beilby, at that time the only engraver in Newcastle. Beilby's fourteen-year-old apprentice gradually took to wood-engraving in his master's workshop because Beilby himself had neither aptitude nor liking for it.

With obvious pride, Bewick declares that he 'was never

a pupil to any drawing master, and had not even a lesson from William Beilby, or his brother Thomas, who along with their other profession, were also drawing masters'. Apprenticeship to Ralph Beilby did, however, bring Bewick into contact with a gifted family which must have influenced his development.

In our day the name of Beilby is well known to connoisseurs of English domestic glass for pieces exquisitely painted in enamel colours, mainly, at any rate, by Ralph's brother and sister, William and Mary. Although enamel painting on glasses in Europe dates back to the fifteenth century, it was first successfully attempted in England by the Beilbys who developed a rococo style of their own. Beilby glasses in the Victoria and Albert Museum exhibit various types of decoration: rococo ornament in a faintly pink white, heraldic devices in polychrome, and vine leaves, tendrils and clusters of grapes in a pale turquoise.

The father of these Beilbys had been a jeweller and silversmith at Durham, where he failed in 1760 and moved to Gateshead. Of his five sons and two daughters, no less than four sons and one daughter are known to have taken to design and crafts. Richard Beilby served his apprenticeship to a die-sinker or seal engraver in Birmingham, where William, too, had learnt enamelling. Ralph worked as a jeweller with his father and afterwards joined Richard in seal-cutting, but Richard died shortly before Bewick's apprenticeship to Ralph. In the *Memoir* Bewick, who had fallen out with Ralph after many years of partnership, describes his master as an oustanding silver engraver: 'In this, as far as I am able to judge, he was one of the best in the Kingdom. . . .'. The Beilbys fascinatingly evoke that world of artisan taste and skill by which the age of elegance was so largely created. How would Bewick's shade have received the news that a Beilby glass was sold for £1,820 in 1960?

Perhaps some of Ralph's silver engraving enjoys an

anonymous survival. Two attractive specimens from Bewick's workshop are known: a salver in the Victoria and Albert Museum and a cake-basket in the museum of Lloyd's. The salver has actually been identified from an entry in one of Bewick's account books, but the cake-basket can confidently be ascribed to his workshop. Both bear the Newcastle hall-mark.

The Newcastle of Bewick's youth was a medieval walled city with gates and towers, dominated by the lantern spire of St Nicholas's Church, now the Cathedral, which appears so often in Bewick's engravings. Gateshead was linked with Newcastle by a bridge over the Tyne dating back to the fourteenth century, and, like old London Bridge, flanked by houses and shops. Ralph Beilby's workshop was in St Nicholas's churchyard. As partners, he and Bewick moved in 1795 to a ramshackle seventeenth-century house at the churchyard's south-east corner. Neither workshop survives, but a commemorative tablet and a replica of E. H. Baily's bust of Bewick mark the site of the later one, demolished in 1902.

Coal, the city's main business, led to the establishment of glass manufacture which has a long history in Newcastle. The Beilbys decorated locally produced wares. Newcastle had had an assay office since the middle of the seventeenth century and some of her silversmiths were excellent craftsmen. Bewick began and ended his career as an artist-tradesman, a miscellaneous engraver specializing in wood-engraving, but the wood-engraved illustrations which brought him fame were, in fact, the astonishing by-products of the workshop in St Nicholas's churchyard, through which flowed a medley of jobs, such as coffin and door plates, sword blades, silver plate, bar bills, tradesmen's cards, bank notes, seals, clock-faces, invitation cards, and the metal moulds into which glass bottles were blown. This eighteenth century *milieu* of skilled, laborious craftsmanship tended to evince the puritanism conspicuous in Hogarth, Benjamin Franklin, and Cobbett. Bewick himself was very much Hogarth's 'Industrious Prentice'.

His beginnings as a wood-engraver were encouraged by Newcastle's prosperous printing industry, then said to enjoy a trade in children's books larger than that of any town outside London. At the end of his seven years apprenticeship Bewick was awarded a prize and medal by the Society of Arts for specimens of wood-engraving which Beilby had submitted on his behalf. Some of these earlier illustrations have a lyrical beauty which Bewick never quite recaptured in his mature work. In particular that very rare book, *Select Fables* (1776), affords an enchanting aspect of Bewick's illustration that has inevitably been neglected. As a youth, he was primarily occupied with illustrations to chapbooks, those booklets largely sold from pedlars' packs. John Newbery, the leading publisher of eighteenth-century chapbooks, who employed Goldsmith and is portrayed in *The Vicar of Wakefield*, did much to raise standards of illustration and production. Bewick graduated from chapbooks to the major works for which he is known, and in the process brought wood-engraving to a level of excellence far beyond that of his precursors, for prints from wood had long been regarded as a cheap form of illustration and had, in consequence, tended to degenerate into crude hack-work.

In his leisure time Bewick found access to books, cultivated physical fitness, and reflected on the conduct of life as viewed by a youthful puritan. It was a stalwart young man, six feet tall and an indefatigable walker, who emerged from his apprenticeship and during 1776–7 took a *wanderjahr* comprising a long tramp through part of the Highlands and an abortive stay in London, of which he shared Cobbett's detestation. For twenty years, from 1777 until 1797, he was in partnership with Ralph Beilby. After he came back from London, Bewick's life was uneventful, except for the work which brought him wide fame.

There appears to be no record of the date at which he began to rent his 'cot' at the Forth, a five-roomed house with a pleasant garden. The Forth was a rural area of Newcastle, now occupied by the central railway station, where Bewick lived from about 1780 until 1812. It was a bachelor establishment up to the date of his marriage in 1786 to Isabella Elliot whom he had known since child-hood. The 'cot' then became a family home where three daughters and an only son grew up. The son, Robert Elliot Bewick (1788–1849), was apprenticed to his father, but was completely overshadowed by him and further handicapped by ill-health. The *Memoir* tells us nothing about a home to which the Bewicks became much attached. Robert Robinson, author of *Thomas Bewick* (1887), who knew Bewick's daughters, mentions 'the large garden' and an apple tree bearing golden pippins, beneath which 'they often took tea and had their evening meal'. When in 1812 he failed to buy the house when it was put up for sale, Bewick moved to 19 West Street, Gateshead, where he died in 1828. Two of his three daughters, Jane and Isabella, lived on there into their nineties and into a new world, dying unmarried in 1881 and 1883.

The remnant of Bewick's birthplace at Cherryburn is the only building, where he lived or plied his trade, which has survived. As for the changed face of Newcastle, its population of 28,294 at the time of the first census in 1801 had multiplied ten-fold to 286,255 by 1931.

A General History of Quadrupeds (1790) and the two volumes of *History of British Birds, Land Birds* (1797) and *Water Birds* (1804), were popularizations of natural history comparable with Gilbert White's *Selborne* (1789). It is significant that White's classic appeared a year earlier than the *Quadrupeds*. Bewick and White, the former by his wood-engravings, the latter by the charm of his writing, did more than any other Englishmen to popularize the study of natural history. Bewick, incidentally, wrote that he 'was much pleased with White's History of Selborne'. These books mark a culminating point in the enthusiasm for natural history which the eighteenth century had inherited from such notably scientific precursors in the seventeenth century as John Ray, and from the enquiring spirit fostered by the foundation in 1660 of the Royal Society (for Improving Natural Knowledge). During the eighteenth century, the age of Lamarck, Linnaeus, Buffon, and Cook's voyages, natural history became a popular pursuit for cultivated men of means and leisure. White himself, Thomas Pennant, and Daines Barrington, exemplify this trend. The names of others occur in the *Memoir*, where Bewick writes of ornithologists with whom his books brought him into touch. Ralph Beilby was mainly responsible for the text of the *Quadrupeds* and for that of the first volume of the *Birds*, although he had help from Bewick. Bewick wrote the text for the second volume, *Water Birds*, after he had acrimoniously dissolved his partnership with Beilby, but he received help from others, such as the Rev Henry Cotes, Vicar of Bedlington.

The pictorial study of natural history has, of course, been revolutionized by photography's resources: telescopic lenses, high speed exposures, and direct colour and slow motion films. A distinguished modern authority, Sir Peter Chalmers Mitchell (1864–1945), thus assessed the ornithological value of Bewick's wood-engravings for the *Birds*: 'some of the figures were drawn from stuffed specimens and accordingly perpetuate the imperfections of the original; others represent species with which the artist was not familiar, and these are either wanting in expression or are caricatures. This is especially observable in the birds of prey . . . but those that were drawn from live birds, or represent species which he knew in life, are worthy of all praise.'

Artistically, figures such as that of the willow wren (*Land Birds*, 1797, p. 222) are a joy for ever, but in our day Bewick's most memorable and original achievement is to be found in the minute tailpieces which he introduced into the *Quadrupeds* and the *Birds*. The figures for the *Quadrupeds* suffer by comparison with those for the *Birds* because many exotic animals could only be drawn from illustrations in existing books, although the long-tailed field-mouse or a breed of dog which Bewick knew well, appear, by contrast, to be vividly depicted. Bewick felt his way to the engraving of figures and tailpieces by making preliminary drawings, many of them in watercolour. The British Museum's splendid Bewick collection includes a series of tiny watercolour drawings for tailpieces which go far to explain the intense life which he could infuse into the correspondingly minute engravings. He combined a keenly concentrated mastery of a subject with genius for design. The more or less oval shapes of his tailpieces can be marvels of felicitously filled space. Bewick's gradations from black to white in different types of wood-engravings are wonderfully handled, as, for instance, in rendering effects of misty rain or snow scenes, where varying greys contribute largely to the weather he could so vividly convey from his mind's eye to the surface of the wood block.

Even more than the rest of Bewick's work, the tailpieces have an unmistakably English flavour and their subjects convey a great variety of moods: pastoral, droll, macabre, and admonitory. There is a world of difference between two subjects in *Land Birds* (1797), the tranquil landscape with cows (p. 74) and the cruel carter whom a fiend is whipping in his cart which the ill-used horse has brought to a stop beneath a gallows (p. 110).* Occasionally, Bewick indulged in rustic crudities, thereby invoking Ruskin's

* [See pp. 102 and 119.]

stern disapproval, who wrote of his 'perpetually increasing wonder at the fixed love of *ugliness* in the British soul which renders the collective works of three of our greatest men—Hogarth, Bewick, and Cruikshank—totally unfit for the sight of women and children, and fitter for the furniture of gaols and pigstyes than of the houses of gentlemen and gentlewomen'. Except for the partially lost lyrical vein of his youth, Bewick can be said to have given all that he had to the figures and tailpieces for the *Birds*. If the figures have inevitably become less important and could not, any-how, afford him the same freely inventive scope as the tail-pieces, their charm is sometimes notably enhanced by the backgrounds against which Bewick placed them. The tame duck is set in what is virtually a delightful landscape tail-piece. The redbreast presides unsentimentally over a bleakly chilly landscape under deep snow.

When, after his abortive stay of nine months in London, Bewick turned his back on the prospect of a career there, he attached his genius to something that has, to some extent, endured. As well as churches and castles, humbler vestiges of his Tyneside remain. There are farmsteads and cottages, sturdily built in heavy stone, which he would have known. An explorer of the Bewick country can, in our day, bring tailpieces to life, as he stands on the river bank near Bywell Castle or surveys Bewickian farms from the windows of a train travelling between Newcastle and Corbridge. Bewick's skill in evoking the plumage of birds was equalled by his knack of rendering the very texture of buildings. Cherryburn was thatched and there was evidently a fair amount of thatch in Bewick's day, but although the heavy stone tiles of so many tailpiece roofs have, to a large ex-tent, been replaced by slates, enough of the former are left to retain fully the character of what he depicted. The Tyne itself, in the stretch between Ovingham and Coxbridge, is not so greatly changed since the time when it inspired him with tailpieces of anglers, a favourite subject because he was himself a keen fisherman. Nor did he fail to draw inspiration from 'the coaly Tyne' and its harsh colliery landscape, as, for instance, in the tailpiece (*Water Birds,* 1804, p. 225), with one of the great flat-bottomed boats, known as 'keels', in the foreground. Keels, used for carrying coal, were painted black to suit their grimy employment, and the keelmen who manned these craft were a race apart, with their own way of life.

The droll moods of the tailpieces are often associated with farmyard livestock and dogs: perhaps a procession of eight geese, who have crossed a stream, leaving a row of stepping-stones behind them, or one of a litter of piglets hesitantly confronting a turkey cock. Morbid and macabre contrasts in several tailpieces point to such streaks in Bewick's nature, for it is evident from the *Memoir* that he was much pre-occupied with the idea of death. His turn for moralizing found grim expression in the Bewick devil, a recurring participant in tailpieces of an admonitory character, who is often associated with gallows or gibbets. The grotesque and macabre flavour imparted to such tailpieces is comparable with the fancies in which the medieval carver—especially of misericords—would sometimes indulge. By and large, these minute wood-engravings afford a fascinating record, mainly bucolic, of everyday existence in the Tyne valley during the latter part of the eighteenth century, which can be likened to the Luttrell Psalter's pictures of English fourteenth century peasants.

Bewick's last considerable work, published in 1818, was *The Fables of Aesop and Others.* Less successful than the *Birds*, it was also poorly printed by Edward Walker of Newcastle, although the same printer had made an excellent job of the second volume of the *Birds*, issued in 1804. Bewick's moralizing impulses, to which he appears to have succumbed progressively as he grew older, are very much in evidence here. The book had a 'preface dedicatory', addressed 'To the Youth of the British Isles', who were exhorted to profit by 'some of the prudential maxims and moral apothegms of the ancient sages'.

The eighteenth century delighted in fables and Bewick was one of a succession of writers and illustrators to contribute to the art that La Fontaine had popularized. In 1727 John Gay, now chiefly remembered for *The Beggars' Opera*, published *Fifty-one Fables in Verse*. Thomas Saint, a Newcastle printer from whom the young Bewick obtained many wood-engraving commissions, published in 1779 *Fables by the Late Mr Gay*, with illustrations engraved by Bewick some years earlier and before he had emerged from his apprenticeship. Samuel Croxall, Archdeacon of Salop and Canon of Hereford, achieved immense success with his *Fables of Aesop and Others*, which had appeared in 1722. By 1825 this book had gone through as many as twenty-two editions. No doubt Bewick hoped that his new venture would prove as successful as the *Birds*.

There are fine things in the *Aesop*, such as 'The Proud Frog and the Ox', but its illustrations are too often stilted because they were not sufficiently derived from the keen observation evinced in the *Birds*. And when it came to 'Jupiter and the Camel' or 'Mercury and the Carver', Bewick had wandered too far from his native heath. Some of the tailpieces are obviously by other hands and few can stand comparison with those for the *Birds*.

It is difficult to say how far Bewick was helped by his pupils. John Jackson (1801–48), a prejudiced witness who had, like a good many others, fallen foul of Bewick, collaborated with W. A. Chatto in *A Treatise on Wood Engraving*. In this volume Jackson chiefly advanced the claims of Robert Johnson and Luke Clennell. They were probably the most gifted of Bewick's pupils and the account of Johnson in the *Memoir* is particularly interesting. Jackson alleged, on the evidence of one of Bewick's early pupils whom he did not name, that of six tailpieces in the first volume of the *Birds* and thirty-nine in the second, some were wholly executed by pupils, others either designed or engraved by them. When, however, these claims are related to the totals of ninety-one tailpieces in the first and a hundred and thirty-six in the second volume, they do not seem to amount to very much. There is evidence, however, that Bewick could be far from generous in his treatment of apprentices. He venomously and anonymously mentions (see p. 88) a court case involving Robert Johnson. The Earl of Bute saw some drawings in the Beilby-Bewick workshop which Johnson had made in his spare time, and was so attracted by them that he spent £30 on buying some. Beilby and Bewick appropriated this money on the ground that the drawings of an apprentice were their property. Johnson's friends brought an action for the recovery of the sum from Beilby and Bewick which succeeded, costs of £9 10s. 11d. being awarded against the partners on April 29, 1795.

In later life, Bewick became acquainted with John F. M. Dovaston (1782–1854), a Shropshire country gentleman interested in natural history, literature, and music. Thirty-six letters from Bewick to Dovaston (British Museum, Egerton MSS. 3147 and 3148) add biographical information to what is otherwise recorded of Bewick as a septuagenarian. Bewick and his daughters, Jane and Isabella, stayed at Buxton Spa during the spring of 1825. Mrs Bewick had died in February of that year after a long and painful illness. Bewick never seems to have recovered fully from the months of strain imposed by his wife's sufferings and was recommended to drink the waters at Buxton as a cure for weakness following an attack of gout in the stomach. Dovaston joined them at the spa and later contributed an article to *The Magazine of Natural History*

(March, 1830) which includes this amusing recollection of their stay:

'There were three windows in the front room, the ledges and shutters whereof he had pencilled all over with funny characters, as he saw them pass to and fro visiting the well. These people were the source of great amusement, the probable histories of whom, and how they came by their ailings, he would humorously narrate, and sketch their figures and features in one instant of time. I have seen him draw a striking likeness on his thumb-nail in one moment, wipe it off with his tongue, and instantly draw another. We dined occasionally at the public table; and one day, over the wine, a dispute arose between two gentlemen about a bird, but was soon terminated by the one affirming he had compared it with the figure and description of Bewick, to which the other replied that Bewick was next to nature. Here the old gentleman seized me by the thigh with his very hand-vice of a grasp, and contrived to keep up the shuttlecock of conversation playfully to his highest satisfaction, though they who praised him so ardently little imagined whose ears imbibed all their honest incense.'

There are two other memorable pen-portraits of Bewick, one by John Jackson in *A Treatise on Wood Engraving* and another by the famous American artist-naturalist, John James Audubon (1780–1851), whose *Ornithological Biography* describes a visit during 1827 to Bewick's house in Gateshead. The best physical likeness of Bewick seems to be the marble bust by E. H. Baily, RA, belonging to Newcastle's Literary and Philosophical Society, for which it was commissioned in 1826 by a body of subscribers 'esteeming the character of Mr Thomas Bewick, whose various *unique* Works reflect so much Honour on himself and on the town of Newcastle-upon-Tyne'. In 1901 the Newcastle Public Library acquired the fine Bewick collection bequeathed by J. W. Pease, the city's principal Bewick memorial.

When he died at Gateshead on November 8, 1828, the influence Bewick was destined to wield had only begun to be felt, mainly through his pupils, former apprentices like William Harvey and Ebenezer Landells, John Jackson, and Luke Clennell, who moved to London, where more and more large publishing concerns were becoming established. The technical virtuosity of Bewick and his school, too evident latterly, as in some of the engravings for the *Aesop* of 1818, with engraving that tends to be over-refined, was adapted to the prolonged era of facsimile wood-engraving which some of Bewick's pupils helped to launch. It was not until the early twentieth century, after the photo-engraving processes had superseded the wood block as the primary method of printing illustrations, that Bewick's influence could yield more fruitful inspiration. The revival of creative wood-engraving, beginning shortly before the first world war, throve successfully after the Society of Wood Engravers had been founded in 1920. Among pioneers of that revival were Bewick devotees, such as Robert Gibbings and Gwendolen Raverat. In any event, there was no wood-engraver of anything like Bewick's stature, to whom the twentieth-century revival could look back. Modern disciples of Bewick are faithful to his predilection for the small block, and it is arguable that wood-engraving is essentially a miniature medium, seen at its best on a small scale. In this connection, it is worth noting that Bewick's rare attempts at engraving large blocks were, in general, much less successful.

It would be easy, in the light of the twentieth century's creative achievement on wood, to dismiss too brusquely the long reign of facsimile wood-engraving. It was uncreative and the engraver's sheer accomplishment could be abominably perverted, as—to take an extreme case—in reproducing a daguerreotype portrait. Nevertheless, it multiplied much that became part of the national consciousness: Tenniel's *Alice*, Du Maurier's drawings for *Punch*, Millais' wonderful book illustrations, and history recorded pictorially in *The Illustrated London News* or *The Graphic*.

A Memoir of Thomas Bewick, Written by Himself was not published by his eldest daughter Jane until 1862, thirty-four years after his death. The autograph manuscript is in the British Museum (Add. MSS. 41481). The text of the *Memoir* presents a difficult problem because Jane Bewick's editing was neither judicious nor literate. 'The Memorial Edition' of Bewick's works (five volumes) was edited by Austin Dobson and published in 1887. It included the *Memoir*, to which Dobson restored much, but not all, that Jane Bewick had excluded. Dobson, for instance, withheld scandalous recollections, such as one naming prominent Newcastle contemporaries of Bewick who 'fell victims to *the Bottle*'. Selwyn Image, at one time Slade Professor at Oxford, arranged for a re-publication of the *Memoir* in 1924. This was merely a reprint of Jane Bewick's version, to which Image added an (unsatisfactory) introduction but nothing by way of explanatory notes. The *Memoir* is little known because, although Austin Dobson added useful notes to his edition, it has never been presented in a form that would make it sufficiently intelligible to the ordinary educated reader. Bewick was a natural but unpractised writer, inclined sometimes to forget that the reader would require more explanation than was forthcoming. Written during the 1820s, the *Memoir* was addressed by Bewick to his daughter Jane. In November, 1827, a year before his death, Bewick wrote to Dovaston that the 'winter's nights (when the spirit moves me) will easily see an end to it. This memoir was first undertaken as [*sic*] the request of Jane Bewick. But for that request I should never have troubled my head about any such thing. The manuscript copy is hers and she seems very unwilling that I should publish it *in my lifetime*. I think her wrong in this for several reasons; but as I feel indifferent about it I can easily be put off.' Study of Bewick's manuscript reveals that he died without revising what he had written during the last months of his life. Later chapters contain passages in which he lapsed into unintelligibility.

When Jane Bewick prepared her father's manuscript for the printer she committed, among other errors, the extraordinary one of omitting almost all that he wrote about his pupils, especially the very interesting account of Robert Johnson. The abridged text here presented derives from collation of Austin Dobson's version of 1887 with the manuscript in the British Museum, a task admirably performed by Miss Irene Calverley of the Cresset Press. Nothing of autobiographical interest is omitted from this edition, but what seemed to be either tedious or obscure has been excluded. Bewick's own footnotes, frequently trivial, have largely been discarded.

Bewick inevitably discussed wood-engraving in his autobiography, but without explaining it for the benefit of readers knowing nothing of the craft's technique.

There are two principal methods by which *relief* prints can be obtained by applying paper under pressure to the worked surface of an inked wood-block. Woodcut, the earlier type of print from wood, was wrought by cutting away with a knife from a block of relatively soft wood the parts of a design not intended to yield an impression on paper when the block was inked and printed. A woodcut block was, in effect, a stamp on which the lines of the design to be printed were carved in relief. Wood-engraving, an early eighteenth century innovation, is wrought with tools similar to those of a metal engraver on a specially hard surface which is normally the end grain of boxwood. The parts of the block's surface not intended to yield an impression are removed in minute shavings by the sharp point of the steel graver. Apart from the greater fineness of wood-engraving, it involves a basic conception different from woodcut, for the wood-engraver is primarily cutting to produce white lines, whereas the maker of a woodcut wrought to produce black lines. Wood-engraving is the more creative craft. The designer's own work on the block is required for the complete expression of his concept in terms of the wood surface. It is generally agreed that Dürer and Holbein—to cite the two greatest names associated with prints from wood—designed for woodcut but did not themselves cut the blocks. Woodcut was the earliest of the reproductive processes by which illustrations could be printed in conjunction with type. Until the invention of photographic engraving, with its line and half-tone block, the wood-block reigned supreme because it could go through the printing press with type, whereas illustrations from copper-plate engravings or etchings had to be printed in a different press. Bewick himself bedevils the distinction between wood-engraving and woodcut by writing of 'cuts' when he means engravings.

There can be no doubt that Bewick is at his best in describing his life from childhood to early manhood. The most vivid pictures of himself begin with the hardy, unruly urchin of Cherryburn, too often in hot water at home and at school. When the scene shifts to Newcastle and his apprenticeship years, he furnishes a fascinating contribution to social history. The account of his *wanderjahr* presents a contrast between the vast enjoyment he derived from his long journey on foot through parts of the Highlands and the dislike he acquired for London and Londoners during a stay there of some nine months. Highlanders attracted him as much as Cockneys repelled him.

As for the character that emerges from the *Memoir*,

few indeed are the autobiographers who have sternly attempted objective self-portraiture. Study of Bewick's life beyond the *Memoir* reveals a cantankerous and suspicious nature. He seems to have had a temperament very different from that of his younger brother John Bewick, a delightful illustrator of children's books, who had been apprenticed to his elder brother and died young. As illustrator and wood-engraver, John is not comparable with his brother, but he could infuse into his work for children's books a charm, reflecting his winning disposition and generous impulses, evidence of which can be found in his letters.

Thomas Bewick, puritan liberal and rural conservative —as is very apparent from his comments in the *Memoir* on aspects of the agrarian revolution—loved to preach. He indulged this proclivity much too heavily in the *Memoir* at the expense of his gift for fascinating reminiscence. The Rev Thomas Hugo (1820–1876), an ardent but undiscriminating collector of Bewick's work, commented acidly on that aspect of the autobiography: 'But I think that most readers of the *Memoir* will agree with me in regretting that the chapters on religious and political matters were not omitted. It is the artist-life of Thomas Bewick which one desires to possess, not his opinions upon subjects on which he was and could be no authority.' All the same, at this distance of time, what Bewick had to say of Pitt, revolutionary France and America, parliamentary reform, and agrarian enclosures, is historically interesting. The same may be said of his views on such themes as the education of boys or the severity of the game laws in his day. Ruskin persuaded Carlyle to read the *Memoir*, and the latter wrote: 'Peace to Bewick: not a great man at all; but a very true of his sort, a well completed and a very *enviable*,—living there in communion with the skies and brooks, not here in ditto with the London Fogs, the roaring witch-mongeries, and railway yellings and howlings.' This characteristic explosion typifies the very worst of Carlyle, who had no feeling for the visual arts and failed to discern that Bewick spent most of his life toiling in the workshop in St Nicholas's Churchyard.

Bewick was hard-featured, had very dark eyes, and seems, judging from portraits painted during his last years, to have looked like a sturdy old farmer. His delight in the Northumbrian *patois* was expressed in two sketches, *The Howdy* (midwife) and *The Upgetting*, which Bewick composed in 'the Teyne Seyde Dialect'. Dovaston mentions his 'extraordinary power of whistling', revealing an acute ear and a strong musical memory. Jackson's pen-portrait, in the *Treatise on Wood-Engraving*, records an apprentice's recollections of the workshop Bewick: 'He used frequently to whistle when at work, and he was seldom without a large quid of tobacco in his mouth. The prominence occasioned by the quid, which he kept between his under lip and his teeth, and not in his cheek, is indicated in most of his portraits.'

There is a great dearth of biographical literature relating to craftsmen, especially in the shape of autobiography. The *Memoir* puts Bewick into an exceedingly small company, along with Benvenuto Cellini and Eric Gill. He has in these introductory pages been described as an artist-tradesman. Dying at the age of seventy-five in 1828, Bewick outlived the artist-tradesman era, surviving into its twilight. We may almost regard his autobiography as that of the last artist-tradesman, although his fame was due to his success as an artist-naturalist. Further, his origin and upbringing place him, with Burns and Millet, in another small company, that of peasant genius.

MEMOIR OF THOMAS BEWICK

CHAPTER I

Introductory — Parentage — Birth, 1753 — Mickley School — Ovingham School — First attempts at drawing —Hunting parties — Sheep — Shelter for sheep in snow storms — Birds — Border songs and laments — Earl of Derwentwater — Whins food for cattle.

Tynemouth, November 1822

MY DEAR JANE,

It is in compliance with your wish that I have, after much hesitation and delay, made up my mind to give you some account of my life, as it may at a future day amuse you and your brother and sisters in your passage through the crooked as well as the pleasant paths of the world. I will commence by giving you some account of your pedigree as far back as I can.

My grandfather, Thomas Bewick, farmed the lands of Painshaw Field and Birches Neuk, near Bywell, and also the Colliery on Mickley Bank, or Mickley Common—how long since I know not, but it might probably be about the year 1700. He had the character of being one of the most intelligent, active, and best farmers on Tyneside, and it was said that, by his good management and great industry, he became very rich; but, except his being an expert angler, I know very little more about him. My grandmother's maiden name was Agnes Arthur, the daughter of a laird of

1

that name at Kirkheaton, where my father was born in the year 1715, while his mother was there (I believe) on a visit to her friends.

My maternal grandfather, Thomas Wilson, and my grandmother, whose maiden name was Hannah Thompson, lived at Ainstable, in Cumberland; but whether he was curate of the parish of that place, or parish clerk, I do not know. It is certain, however, that he was one or the other, and that he taught a school there; and, from the circumstance of his teaching his sons, and some of his daughters, Latin, I conclude he taught some of his scholars the same language. When he died, his eldest son, Christopher, became possessed of his freehold property, consisting of a house, etc., and a few fields adjoining. The rest of his family were left little beside a good education, and were spread abroad in the world to do the best they could for themselves. In this state of their affairs, my mother, Jane, and her youngest sister, Hannah, were taken by a distant relation, a Mrs Gregson, of Appleby, to remain with her until she could get them places to live at. About this time, the Rev Christopher Gregson had been appointed to the curacy of Ovingham, and wanted a housekeeper; and my mother, though young, was thought able to undertake that office, and accordingly engaged to perform it,

Your maternal grandfather's name was Robert Elliot, and your grandmother's Jane Forster. He farmed the land of Woodgate, near Bill Quay, where your mother was born. He afterwards removed to a farm at Ovingham, where he died in 1777, leaving the character of a sensible, honest, and industrious man.

How long my mother lived with Mr Gregson, before her marriage, I know not; but from him I afterwards learned that she was a valuable servant to him, both with respect to his house-keeping concerns, and for the occasional assistance she afforded him in hearing his pupils their

2

Latin tasks. From Ovingham, in the year 1752, she married my father, and went to live with him at Cherryburn House, near the small village or hamlet of Eltringham, where all their family, of which I was the eldest, were born. The family consisted of myself and brothers, John and William; and my sisters, Hannah, Agnes, Ann, Sarah, and Jane. Sarah died at the age of 16; the rest were reared to maturity, and were sent off, one way or another, into the world.

In August 1753 I was born, and was mostly entrusted to the care of my aunt Hannah (my mother's sister), and my grandmother, Agnes Bewick; and the first thing I can remember was, that the latter indulged me in everything I had a wish for; or, in other words, made me a great pet. I was not to be 'snubbed' (as it was called), do what I would; and, in consequence of my being thus suffered to have my own way, I was often scalded and burnt, or put in danger of my breaking my bones by falls from heights I had clambered up to.

The next circumstance, which I well remember, was that of my being sent to Mickley School when very young; and this was not done so much with a view to my learning, as to keep me out of 'harm's way'. I was some time at this school without making much progress in learning my letters or spelling small words; the master, perhaps, was instructed not to keep me very close at my book; but, in process of time, he began to be more and more severe upon me; and I see clearly at this day, that he frequently beat me when faultless, and also for not learning what it was not in my power to comprehend. Others suffered in the same way. He was looked upon as a severe or 'cross' man, and did not spare his rod. His name I do not recollect; but he was nicknamed 'Shabby Rowns'. He was a tall, thin man; and, with a countenance severe and grim, he walked about the school-room, with the tawse or a switch in his hand.

He, no doubt, thought he was keeping the boys to their lessons, while the jabbering and noise they made was enough to stun anyone, and impressed the people passing by with the idea that Bedlam was let loose. How long he went on in this way I do not recollect; but, like many others of his profession, who were at that time appointed to fill the most important office of a teacher, no pains had been taken to enquire whether he possessed the requisite qualifications befitting him for it. He went on with a senseless system of severity, where ignorance and arrogance were equally conspicuous. Conduct like this sours the minds of some boys, renders others stupid, and serves to make all more or less disgusted with learning. Upon some occasion or other, he ordered me to be flogged; and this was to be done by what was called 'hugging', that is, by mounting me upon the back of a stout boy, who kept hold of my hands over his shoulders, while the posteriors were laid bare, where he supposed he could do the business freely. In this instance, however, he was mistaken; for, with a most indignant rage, I sprawled, kicked, and flung, and, I was told, bit the innocent boy on the neck, when he instantly roared out, and flung me down; and, on my being seized again by the old man, I rebelled, and broke his shins with my iron-hooped clogs, and ran off. By this time, the boy's mother, who was a spirited woman, and lived close by, attracted by the ferment that was raised, flew (I understood) into the school-room, when a fierce scold ensued between the master and her. After this I went no more to his school, but played the truant every day, and amused myself by making dams, and swimming boats in a small burn which ran through a place then called the 'Colliers' Close Wood', till the evening, when I returned home with my more fortunate or more obedient schoolfellows.

How long it was before my absence from school was discovered I know not, but I got many severe beatings

4

from my father and mother, in the interval between my leaving school and the old master's death. As soon as another schoolmaster (James Burn) was appointed, I was sent to him; and he happened to be of a directly opposite character to the late one. With him I was quite happy, and learned as fast as any other of the boys, and with as great pleasure. After the death of this much respected young man, who lived only a very few years after his appointment, my learning any more at Mickley School was at an end.

Some time after this, my father put me to school under the care of the Rev C. Gregson, of Ovingham; and well do I remember the conversation that passed between them on this occasion. It was little to my credit; for my father began by telling him that I was so very unguidable that he could not manage me, and he begged of my new master that he would undertake that task, and they both agreed that 'to spare the rod was to spoil the child'. This precept was, I think, too severely acted upon, sometimes upon trivial occasions and sometimes otherwise.

I was for some time kept at reading, writing, and figures—how long, I know not, but I know that as soon as my question was done upon my slate, I spent as much time as I could find in filling with my pencil all the unoccupied spaces, with representations of such objects as struck my fancy; and these were rubbed out, for fear of a beating, before my question was given in. As soon as I reached fractions, decimals, etc., I was put to learn Latin, and in this I was for some time complimented by my master for the great progress I was making; but, as I never knew for what purpose I had to learn it, and was wearied out with getting off long tasks, I rather flagged in this department of my education, and the margins of my books, and every space of spare and blank paper, became filled with various kinds of devices or scenes I had met with; and these were often accompanied with wretched rhymes explanatory of

5

them. As soon as I filled all the blank spaces in my books, I had recourse, at all spare times, to the gravestones and the floor of the church porch, with a bit of chalk, to give vent to this propensity of mind of figuring whatever I had seen. At that time I had never heard of the word 'drawing'; nor did I know of any other paintings beside the king's arms in the church, and the signs in Ovingham of the Black Bull, the White Horse, the Salmon, and the Hounds and Hare. I always thought I could make a far better hunting scene than the latter: the others were beyond my hand. I remember once of my master overlooking me while I was very busy with my chalk in the porch, and of his putting me very greatly to the blush by ridiculing and calling me a conjuror. My father, also, found a deal of fault for 'misspending my time in such idle pursuits'; but my propensity for drawing was so rooted that nothing could deter me from persevering in it; and many of my evenings at home were spent in filling the flags of the floor and the hearthstone with my chalky designs.

After I had long scorched my face in this way, a friend, in compassion, furnished me with some paper upon which to execute my designs. Here I had more scope. Pen and ink, and the juice of the brambleberry, made a grand change. These were succeeded by a camel-hair pencil and shells of colours; and, thus supplied, I become completely set up; but of patterns, or drawings, I had none. The beasts and birds which enlivened the beautiful scenery of woods and wilds surrounding my native hamlet, furnished me with an endless supply of subjects. I now, in the estimation of my rustic neighbours, became an eminent painter, and the walls of their houses were ornamented with an abundance of my rude productions, at a very cheap rate. These chiefly consisted of particular hunting scenes, in which the portraits of the hunters, the horses, and of every dog in the pack, were, in their opinion, *as well as my own*, faithfully delineated. But while I was proceeding in this way, I was at the same time deeply engaged in matters nearly allied to this propensity for drawing; for I early became acquainted, not only with the history and the character of the domestic animals, but also with those which roamed at large.

The conversations of the Nimrods of that day, in which the instincts and peculiar properties of the various wild animals were described in glowing terms, attracted my keenest attention; and to their rude and lengthened narratives I listened with extreme delight. With me they made a winter's evening fly fast away. At holiday times—and at other times when prevented by the floods of the Tyne from getting across it to school—I was sure, with the most ardent glee, to make one of the number in the hunting parties which frequently took place at that time; whether it might be in the chase of the fox or the hare, or in tracing the foumart in the snow, or hunting the badger at midnight. The pursuing, baiting, or killing, these animals, never at any time struck me as being cruel. The mind had not as yet been impressed with the feelings of humanity. This, however, came upon me at last; and the first time I felt the change happened by my having (in hunting) caught the hare in my arms, while surrounded by the dogs and the hunters, when the poor, terrified creature screamed out so piteously—like a child—that I would have given anything to have saved its life. In this, however, I was prevented; for a farmer well known to me, who stood close by, pressed upon me, and desired I would 'give her to him'; and, from his being better able (as I thought) to save its life, I complied with his wish. This was no sooner done than he proposed to those about him, 'to have a bit more sport with her', and this was to be done by first breaking one of its legs, and then again setting the poor animal off a little before the dogs. I wandered away to a little distance, oppressed by my own feelings, and could not join the crew

7

again, but learned with pleasure that their intended victim had made its escape.

The 'musical din' of the hounds still continued to have its charms, and I still continued to follow them; but, from that day forward, I have ever wished that this poor, persecuted, innocent creature might escape with its life. The worrying of foxes, the baiting of foumarts, otters, badgers, etc., did not awaken in me similar feelings; for in the fierce conflicts between them and the dogs, there was something like an exchange of retaliation, and not unfrequently the aggressors were beaten; and I have with pleasure seen that wonderfully courageous animal, the badger (with fair play), beat the dogs of a whole neighbourhood, one after another, completely off.

In the vermin-hunting excursions, in the depth of winter, while the whole face of nature was bound in frost and covered with deep snow, in traversing through bogs, amidst reeds and rushes, I have often felt charmed with the sight of birds—flushed, and sometimes caught, by the terrier dogs—which I had never seen or heard of before; and I am still in doubt whether some of them have not escaped being noticed as British birds.

These were the diversions of the winter months, which I enjoyed in an extreme degree, amidst the storm and the tempest. In that season I was also sometimes better employed in looking after a small flock of sheep on the fell, a part of which was my own. The extremity of the weather had taught them to seek a place of shelter under a steep but low 'brae', overhung with whins,* under which, in such weather, I was almost certain to find them and their associates all huddled together. To this place, through wreaths of snow, I early bent my way, with a bundle of hay on my back, and my pockets sometimes filled with oats, which I distributed amongst them. Upon these occa-

* [Gorse.]

8

sions, though at other times extremely wild, they were quite tame, and seemed to know me.

From my sheep thus drawing into shelter, gave rise to an opinion I formed, and which has been confirmed by long reflection, that much may yet be done to protect the larger flocks from being overblown and lost on the bleak moors, in great snow storms. Were long avenues made by double rows of whin hedges, planted parallel to each other at about six feet asunder, and continued in the form of two sides of a square, with the whins of each side drawn together, and to grow interplatted at the tops, so as to form an arched kind of roof, the sheep would, on instinctively seeing the coming storm, immediately avail themselves of such asylums, and particularly in the lambing season. In the corner of the angle of this square, the shepherd might have his hovel, thatched with heather and ling, and his beds for himself and his dogs, made of the same materials; and the whole of this 'bield' might be rendered so snug as greatly to defy the severity of the winter's drifting blasts and wreaths of snow.

At that time of life, every season had its charms; and I recollect well of listening with delight, from the little window at my bed-head,* to the murmuring of the flooded burn which passed my father's house, and sometimes roused me from my bed, to see what it was like. On such occasions I would have cut a 'shive' from the black sour rye loaf, and gone to bed again to eat it. After this, my first and common employment was to 'muck' the byer; and, when the servant girl did not come soon enough, I frequently tried my hand at milking the cows; and I was always particularly keen of being there in snow storms. When this was the case, within the byer door, I snugly watched the appearance of various birds, which passed the little dean below, and which the severity of the weather drove from

* [Visible on p. 25 to the right of the horse.]

9

place to place, in search of shelter. With the sight of my intimate acquaintances, the robins, wrens, blackbirds, sparrows, a solitary crow, and some others, I was not much attracted, but always felt an extreme pleasure and curiosity in seeing the more rare visitants—such as the woodcock, the snipe, and other waders, with the redwings, fieldfares, etc.—make their appearance.

The winter evenings were often spent in listening to the traditionary tales and songs, relating to men who had been eminent for their prowess and bravery in the border wars, and of others who had been esteemed for better and milder qualities, such as their having been good landlords, kind neighbours, and otherwise in every respect bold, independent, and honest men. I used to be particularly affected with the warlike music, and with the songs relative to the former description of characters; but with the songs regarding the latter, a different kind of feeling was drawn forth, and I was greatly distressed, and often gave vent to it in tears. These songs and 'laments' were commemorative of many worthies; but the most particular ones that I now remember were those respecting the Earl of Derwentwater, who was beheaded in the year 1715, and was looked upon as having been a victim to the cruelty of the reigning family, and who was venerated as a saint upon earth. It was said that the light from Heaven attended his corpse to the vault at Dilston Hall, and that prosperity would shine no more upon Tyneside. Then followed the sorrowful remembrances of those that were dead and gone. To sigh over them was unavailing; they had filled the space allotted to them on this side of Time, and the winds had blown over their silent graves for ages past. The predictions that the mansions of those that remained would soon, for want of heirs, become desolate—these and such like melancholy reflections made a deep impression on my mind; and I have often since, with feelings of extreme regret, beheld these mansions, once the seats of hospitality, dilapidated, and the families which occupied them now become extinct and forgotten.

When the winter began somewhat to abate of its rigours, or in the early spring, it was a common job for me, before setting off to school, to rise betimes in the morning—as indeed I was always accustomed to do—and equipt with an apron, an old dyking mitten, and a sharpened broken sickle, to set off amongst the whin bushes, which were near at hand, to cut off their last year's sprouts. These were laid into a corner till the evening, when I stript, and fell to work to 'cree' them with a wooden 'mell', in a stone trough, till the tops of the whins were beaten to the consistency of soft, wet grass; and, with this mess, I fed the horses before I went to bed, or in the morning as occasion might require. They were shy about eating this kind of provender at first, and I was obliged to mix oats with it; but they soon became so fond of it, alone, that there was no need of any mixture. I know not whether a scarcity of fodder first gave rise to the suggestion of using this expedient, or it was tried as an experiment; but certain it is that this kind of food agreed so well with the horses that they became soon very sleek, and cast their winter coats of hair long before other horses that were fed in the common way. Cows would not eat the whin tops thus prepared, but, in a winter of scarcity, I have known all hands at work cutting ivy from the trees, and even small ash twigs, to be given to the cattle as fodder.

CHAPTER II

FROM the little window at my bed-head, I noticed all the varying seasons of the year; and when the spring put in, I felt charmed with the music of birds, which strained their little throats to proclaim it. The chief business imposed upon me as a task, at this season, was my being set to work to 'scale' the pastures and meadows; that is, to spread the mole-hills over the surface of the ground. This, with gardening, and such like jobs, was very hungry work, and often made me think dinner was long in coming; and, when at last it was sent to me, be it what it might, I sat down on the 'lown' side of a hedge and ate it with a relish that needed no sauce.

As soon as the bushes and trees began to put forth their buds, and make the face of nature look gay—this was the signal for the angler to prepare his fishing tackle. In doing this I was not behind hand. Fishing rods, set gads, and night lines were all soon made fit for use, and with them, late and early, I had a busy time of it, during the summer months, until the frosts of autumn forbade me to proceed. The uneasiness which my late evening wadings by the waterside gave to my father and mother, I have often since reflected upon with regret. They could not go to bed with the hopes of getting to sleep, while haunted with the ap-

12

prehension of my being drowned; and well do I remember to this day my father's well-known whistle, which called me home. He went to a little distance from the house, where nothing obstructed the sound, and whistled so loud, through his finger and thumb, that in the still hours of evening it might be heard echoing up the vale of the Tyne to a very great distance. This whistle I learned to imitate, and answered it as well as I could, and then posted home.

From early in the morning till night, I was scarcely ever out of an action either good or bad; or, when not kept close at school, or in doing jobs such as those I have described, I was almost constantly engaged in some mischievous prank or other; but with a detail of these it would be wearisome to load my narrative; they were occasioned by the overflowings of an active, wild disposition. At one time, in imitation of the savages described in *Robinson Crusoe*— or some other savages—I often, in a morning, set off *stark naked* across the fell, where I was joined by some associates, who, in like manner, ran about like mad things, or like Bedlamites who had escaped. Climbing the tall trees at Eltringham for rook nests, at the hazard of breaking our necks or our bones, was another piece of business which employed our attention. I was also engaged in another equally dangerous. Having formed the resolution of curing a vicious 'runaway' horse belonging to my father, which no one durst mount, I, however, took the opportunity, when out of sight of any of the family, to do so. With my hand entwined in his mane, and bare-backed, I set him a-going, and let him run over 'sykes' and burns, up hill and down hill, until he was quite spent. In a short time I discovered that, to make him run at all, he must be whipt to it. At other times I swam him in the river. This, and such like treatment, made him look ill, and quite tamed him.

I have often since shuddered at the thoughts of doing

these and such like desperate acts, and wondered how I escaped; but neither caution nor fear had at that time taken a place in the mind; on the contrary, any uncommon or frightful exploit had charms in it that I could not resist. One of these pranks, however, attracted the attention of the neighbourhood, brought me into a great dilemma, and occasioned me a severe beating. I engaged a constant associate, Josh. Liddell, who was ever ready at my command to help me, as soon as I communicated any design to him. I had discovered two oxen in a little savannah or bit of grazing ground, surrounded with hazel and other bushes, near the brink of the river. Thither we went in order to enjoy so tempting a sight as to see them plunge overhead into the flood. When all was ready, we suddenly, with long branches in our hands, sprang upon them from the bushes overhanging the precipice, the danger of which they did not see; and they were plunged, with such a *delightful dash*, overhead into the river! They, however, happened to be no worse for it; for they were driven down by the rapid current of the flood, and landed safely at a distance below. This exploit, happening on a Sunday afternoon, was an aggravation of the crime.

After this my father mostly took me with him to church, but while there, except shouting as loud as I could, while the Psalms were singing, there was little to engage my attention. I therefore employed myself in almost constantly drawing various figures upon the soft, painted bookboard with a pin. In doing this, no one noticed me, especially as I held down my head; and, having got the church service off, I repeated it the same as the congregation. This apparently regular behaviour was not, however, of long duration, and was broken in upon at last. Sunday after Sunday a clownish fellow had obtruded himself into our pew. I did not think this quite right, and wished to put an end to it; and this happened in a very rude

14

way in the end. A dumb man ('Dummy, of Wylam'*), a constant church-goer, had a seat in the pew before ours, where, regularly during the service, he fell fast asleep. When in that state, and sitting right before our obtruder, I reached aside, and gave 'Dummy' a smart blow on the head, and instantly, as if I knew nothing of the matter, I seemed to be quite grave, and intent on looking on my prayer book, while the fellow was putting on a broad grin. At this poor Dummy was enraged, and with a distorted countenance, he kept thumping the man on the face and head, at the same time making a hideous noise, which was heightened by the fellow's shouting, and calling him 'fool', at the same time assuring him that it was I who gave the blow, and not he. To the deaf man this was a waste of words. It need not be added that the congregation was greatly disturbed, while perhaps none knew or suspected the cause except my father and my preceptor in the pulpit.

Sometimes the lads in the same class I belonged to, when we had been doing amiss, were sent to cut birch rods to whip us with. At other times we were locked into the belfry, where we often amused ourselves by drawing each other up by the bell ropes to the first floor; but one of our comrades having (by the rope slipping too violently through the hands of those who held it) been precipitated to the ground, by which he was a good deal hurt, that mode of punishment was altogether dropped. It sometimes happened to me to be confined there alone, and once I got up to the top of the steeple. Whether I had ventured a little down on the outside to look for birds' nests I do not remember, but this was asserted by some of the women in the village, who upon this occasion found a deal of fault with the Parson for putting me into a place where such risks were to be run. Poor man, I think he had had a

* [Wylam is about two miles east of Ovingham on the north bank of the Tyne.]

15

troublesome time of it with one or other of us; and I remember well, once in particular, of putting him into very great pain and distress of mind. After a great flood, a large piece of ice, about the size of the floor of a room, had been left in a place called 'Ned's Hole', by the side of the river. This I got upon, and persuaded several others to do the same, and we then set to work with a 'boat-stower' to push it off shore; and, in this manner, we got some distance up the river, opposite to the parsonage garden, where our master happened to be, and saw us. I could see by his agitated motions, and his uplifted hands, that he was put into a state much easier to be felt than described. After having been guilty of misdemeanours of this kind, I did not go back to school for the remainder of the day; but waded, or otherwise crossed, the river, and sat down or amused myself among the bushes on the water banks, until the rest of the scholars left school, when I joined them and went home. But as it would not have been safe for me to go to bed (if conscious of guilt, or if otherwise betrayed) for fear of a visit from my father, I always took up my abode for the night in the byer loft, among the hay or straw, knowing well that, when his passion subsided, I should escape a beating from his hands.

The first cause of my preceptor beginning a severe system of flogging (beside the quantum I received for mischievous acts), was for not getting off my Latin tasks. When this was not done to his mind, he, by way of punishment, gave me another still worse to do, and still longer, till at length I gave up even attempting to get through them at all, and began to stand a flogging without being much put about by it. I think (at this day) my very worthy preceptor, in following this rather indiscriminate system of severe punishments, was wrong. He often beat his own son, a youth of an uncommonly, mild, kind, and cheerful disposition, whom I felt more distressed at seeing punished

16

than if it had been myself; for I mostly considered that I richly deserved the stripes inflicted upon me, and that he did not.

There was a misdemeanour for which, above all the rest, I was more severely punished, both at school and at home, than for any other fault; and that was for fighting with other boys. To put a stop to this practice, was the particular request of my mother. To her it was odious in the extreme. Her reasons I do not forget. She quoted Scripture in support of them. Therein, she said, we were directed, 'if we were struck on one cheek, to turn the other also' (I forget the exact words): but it is a portion of Scripture I did not obey. She also maintained that the business of fighting was degrading to human nature, and put a man that practised it on a level with dogs. I am conscious that I never sought a quarrel with anyone; but I found an insult very bad to bear, and generally in the most secret manner contrived 'to fight it out.'

When the floggings inflicted upon me had in a great measure begun to lose their effect, another mode of punishment was fallen upon; and that was, after the school hours were over, to lock me into the church, where I was kept till the dusk of the evening. This solitary confinement was very irksome to me; as I had not at that time got over a belief in ghosts and boggles, for the sight of which I was constantly upon the look out. Oppressed with fear, I peeped here and there into every corner, in dread of seeing some terrible spirit. In time, however, this abated, and I amused myself, as well as I could, in surveying the surrounding objects, and in climbing up the pillars, with the help of a rope or a handkerchief, as I used to do in getting up large trees. It happened one evening, when my master, as usual, came to let me out, that I was sitting astride upon the capital of one of the pillars, where he did not see me. He called on me, but I made no answer, and he then posted

17

off to see if the door was fast, and having ascertained that it was, he marched along the aisles in great perturbation of mind, frequently exclaiming 'God bless me!', etc. When he was gone, I slipped down, and found the choir door only bolted on the inside, so I waded the river and posted home, and slept in my old asylum, the hay loft. I have frequently bitterly repented of having given a man I afterwards so highly respected through life so much pain and trouble.

I have before noticed that the first time I felt compassion for a dumb animal, was upon my having caught a hare in my arms. The next occurrence of the kind happened with a bird. I had no doubt knocked many down with stones before, but they had escaped being taken. This time, however, the little victim dropped from the tree, and I picked it up. Struck with its beauty, I instantly ran into the house with it. It was alive, and looked me piteously in the face; and, as I thought, could it have spoken, it would have asked me why I had taken away its life. I felt greatly hurt at what I had done, and did not quit it all the afternoon. I turned it over and over, admiring its plumage, its feet, its bill, and every part of it. It was a bullfinch. I did not then know its name, but I was told it was a 'little Matthew Martin'. This was the last bird I killed; but many, indeed, have been killed since on my account.

I had been at man-fights, dog-fights, and cock-fights, without feeling much compassion. Indeed, with the last of these exhibitions, I was more entertained at seeing the wry faces, contortions, and agitations of the clowns who surrounded the cock-pit, or circle, than I was with the cocks fighting. It was long before I felt disgusted at seeing men fight. This, however, happened at last. A travelling merchant, or respectable pedlar—a slim-made, genteel-looking man—had perhaps forgotten himself over a glass, and not minded what company he was in. He could not, however, be long in such society without being insulted;

18

but, be that as it might, a fight ensued, in which the stranger was over-matched. I saw only the concluding part, and was extremely shocked; for the stranger was sitting propped up with his arms behind him, quite spent and speechless, and looked like a corpse. After sitting a short time in this helpless state, his opponent walked coolly up to him, and with a blow on the face or head laid him flat on the ground. I thought he was killed, at which I became so frantic with rage and indignation, that I believe, at the moment, if I had had a pistol at hand, I would have shot the sturdy barbarian.

In going along with my narrative, I have noticed some of the first impressions which produced a change, and left a strong effect on my mind. In some of these, the change was quick and decisive; in others of a more tardy nature; and prejudices which were early rooted were not easily removed. Among the worst, was that of a belief in ghosts, boggles, apparitions, etc. These wrought powerfully upon the fears of the great bulk of the people at that time, and, with many, these fears are not rooted out even at this day. The stories so circumstantially told respecting these phantoms and supernatural things, I listened to with the dread they inspired, and it took many an effort, and I suffered much, before it could be removed. What helped me greatly to conquer fears of that kind was my knowing that my father constantly scouted such idle, or, indeed, such pernicious tales. He would not allow me to plead fear as any excuse, when he had to send me an errand at night; and, perhaps, my being frequently alone in the dark might have the effect of enabling me greatly to rise superior to such weakness.

I have known men, both old and young, who dared to encounter almost any danger, yet *were afraid of their own shadows*: and I remember well of trying the experiment, one night, upon a servant man of my father's, who was a

19

kind of village Caesar, and feared not to stand the most desperate battles with others of the same cast, upon any occasion. I began by sneering at his courage, and then bet him a penny that I durst do what he dared not. All I intended to do I set about rather deliberately, and then rose to perform *my feat*, which was to walk along the dark passage to the back door, and to repeat something (rather ominous, indeed) about 'Silkey' and 'Hedley Kow'. After performing my task, I returned with apparent agitation and fear, and sat down in silence close beside him for some time, and then asked him if he durst do the like. I, however, saw, by his hesitation, that the performance by him was given up, and he only remarked that 'one may soon get what one'll never cast'.

At another time, in broad daylight, I took it into my head to make another trial of this kind upon my father's pitmen. For this purpose I detained our cur dog, until I buckled him up in a pair of old 'sods', which covered him beyond both head and tail, and set him off to the pit, knowing well that he would go straight there; for he was accustomed every day to leave the pit lodge, and go home, where he waited until he saw that dinner was ready, and then his reappearance at the pit was as good as telling my father and his servants to come home. I durst not have thus amused myself if I had not known that my father was out of the way. I set off on the inside of the hedge, keeping pace with the dog all the way up to the pit heap, near which I stopped, and peeped to see the effect that would be produced; and this was really curious. One of the men, seeing the odd appearance of something alive, with a long body, without either legs, head, or tail, moving straight forward towards him, knew not what to make of it; and, after rubbing his eyes, he ran off to his companions, who, when they had taken a peep, all set off, with speed, on their way home.

In a business of a similar kind, which happened not long after, it was my lot to be the sufferer. A few companions used to come at nights to our house to play at cards with me, and I, in turn, visited them for the same purpose. We were, however, taken to task by a bigoted old woman in the neighbourhood, who called the cards the 'devil's books'. She told me one night before setting off to play with my companions, as usual, that, if I looked under the table, I would see the devil; and I recollect that I several times peeped to see if he were indeed there. When we were done playing, two of the gamesters, as was customary, set me across part of the fell towards home. I was, however, much surprised at their suddenly leaving me without saying goodnight, or making any reply to my shouting after them, and they were soon out of sight. This was at a place called the 'Sand Holes', which I then left, and was turning towards home, when, behold! to my utter amazement, I saw the devil! It was a clear moonlight night; I could not be mistaken—his horns—his great white, goggle eyes, and teeth, and tail—his whole person stood fairly before me! As I gazed, I thought the hair lifted the hat on my head. He stood, and I stood, for some time; and, I believe, if he had then come up to me, I must have dropped down. Certain it is, however, that desperation succeeded fear. I moved aside, and he did the same. I involuntarily got my 'jackleg knife', and, if he had then approached me, he to a certainty would have been stabbed. I slipped off my clogs, made a start in a bending direction, and at full speed ran home. He pursued me nearly to the door, but I beat him in the race. I had always understood that any person who had seen a ghost, or evil spirit, would faint on coming into a house with a fire in it. I feared this, but I fainted none! and when my father asked me what was the matter, I told him I had seen the devil. He, perhaps, without thinking, gave me a slap on the head. It was not long, however, till the following affair transpired. The man who personated the devil, when he met me, had been on his way to a 'kirn supper',* and was going in what was called 'a guising'. When my father heard the whole transaction, he wrought himself up into a great rage; and very shortly after, meeting the man (Tom Usher) in the street at Corbridge, who had frightened me, he instantly paid him off by giving him a sound beating. When the people, who always considered my father as a remarkably peaceable man, saw him thus engaged, they expressed their surprise; but, as soon as they heard the reason for what had been done, they were also exasperated, and, I was given to understand, the man was obliged to leave the village.

The first time I took notice of any of my female schoolfellows arose from a reproof I met with, and the manner it was given, from one of them. The amiable person alluded to, was Miss Betty Gregson, my preceptor's daughter, and somewhere about my own age. She kept a messet dog,† and the sleek, fat, useless animal was much disliked by me as well as by some of the other boys. When it made its appearance in the churchyard, which it sometimes did, we set about frightening it; and, for this purpose, some of us met it at every gate and outlet, and stopped its retreat till it became quite distressed. The last time that this kind of sport was practised on her little dog, I happened to be the only actor. Having met with it at a little distance from its home, I had stopped it from entering the house, and had pursued it about and about, or met it at the end of every avenue, till it was put into great 'bodily fear'! This behaviour towards her little favourite was very offensive to Miss Gregson. She could endure it no longer, and she called me to account for it. I can never forget her looks upon the occasion. She no doubt intended to scold

* [A Harvest Festival jollification.]
† [A lap-dog.]

22

me, but the natural sweetness of her disposition soon showed itself in its true colours. She did not know how to scold; for, after some embarrassing attempts at it, and some hesitation, she put me in mind of my being related to her, and of her uniform kindness to me, and with irresistible arguments and persuasions made me see the impropriety of my conduct. With me this left its mark; for from that time forward I never plagued any of the girls at school, nor did anything that might give them offence; nor has this impression ever been effaced from my mind, but has been there fostered through life and settled into a fixed respect and tender regard for the whole sex.

Hitherto my life at school and at home might be considered as a life of warfare, and punishments of various kinds had been inflicted upon me apparently with little effect. As a cure for my misdeeds, my worthy master, however, at length found out a better and more effectual way. He one day invited me to dine with him, and after showing me the greatest kindness, he followed this up in a friendly, plain, and open way by remonstrating with me on the impropriety of my past conduct, the evil tendency of it, and the pain and trouble it had given him; urging me, at the same time, in such a persuasive tone, instantly to desist from it, that I felt quite overpowered with his discourse, and fell into a flood of tears. The result was, I never dared to encounter another of these friendly meetings; and, while I remained at his school, he never again had occasion to find fault with me.

The transactions in which I afterwards became engaged afforded me more real enjoyment. As silent time stole away, in the varied seasons of the long-measured years, changes gradually took place in many of the erroneous notions I had formed of things. As the mind became more expanded, curiosity led me to enquire into the nature of the objects which attracted my attention. Among the first was that of birds, their nests, their eggs, and their young. These to me were long a source of great delight, and many a spring morning I watched and looked after them. I also spent many a summer evening, on my way home from school, lost in wonder in examining the works going forward among a nation of pismires (ants). The place they occupied was on the top of the 'Boat Hill', near Eltringham, and the colony was the largest I had ever seen. From it their narrow roads, through the grass, radiated in various directions to a great distance. These were like as many turnpike roads, and as busily crowded as any among men, leading to or from a great fair. I have sometimes with a stick overturned their accumulated gatherings, when it was curious to observe the effect produced. The greatest bustle and confusion ensued; and yet I have observed with surprise that next morning everything was restored to the same order as before. I noticed that they had other enemies that broke in upon them, and which perhaps injured them more than I did; and these were the turkeys from the village, where great numbers were bred every year. As soon as the young brood were able to walk abroad, the mother led them every day to this great ant hill, where they no doubt made terrible havoc among the inhabitants and their works.

Bees also attracted much of my attention. I could not see into the interior of their works, but I made every inquiry of those who had long kept them, and gathered, in this way, as good a knowledge of their history and economy as I could. One of my morning jobs was to sit before the hives, with a stick like a spatula, to kill the wasps, as they alighted to enter and rob them. I could see the bees enter, loaded with what they had culled from every flower, but never could see them attack or repel their enemies.

I frequently amused myself in observing the murders of a large spider, which had placed its web in the corner of the little window at my bed-head. Being wishful to see how it managed its affairs, I prevented the servant girl from brushing the web away. Its proceedings did not excite in me any favourable opinion. Having seen it seize every innocent fly that set foot upon its snares, I had a mind to try how it would conduct itself towards a more powerful opponent. For this purpose I caught a wasp, which I held by its wings upon the web until its feet got entangled, when out came the hitherto unthwarted tyrant; and, after some apparent hesitation, it at length was tempted to pounce upon the intruder. The struggle was, however, very short. I soon saw the wasp double itself up and dart its sting into the body of its enemy, which instantly retired, and never afterwards returned. This is only one experiment, but further trials of the kind might be made to come at truth.

Esto perpetua

CHAPTER III

CHERRYBURN HOUSE, the place of my nativity, and which for many years my eyes beheld with cherished delight, is situated on the south side of the Tyne, in the county of Northumberland, a short distance from the river. The house, stables, etc., stand on the west side of a little dean, at the foot of which runs a burn. The dean was embellished with a number of cherry and plum trees, which were terminated by a garden on the north. Near the house were two large ash trees growing from one root; and, at a little distance, stood another of the same kind. At the south end of the premises was a spring well, overhung by a large hawthorn bush, behind which was a holly hedge; and further away was a little boggy dean, with underwood and trees of different kinds. Near the termination of this dean, towards the river, were a good many remarkably tall ash trees, and one of oak, supposed to be one of the tallest and straightest in the kingdom. On the tops of these was a rookery, the sable inhabitants of which, by their consultations and cawings, and the bustle they made when building their nests, were among the first of the feathered race to proclaim the approaching spring. The corn-fields and pastures to the eastward were surrounded with very large oak and ash trees. Indeed, at that time, the country between Wylam and Bywell was beautified with a great deal of wood, which presented the appearance of a continued forest; but these are long since stubbed up. Needy gentry care little about the beauty of a country, and part of it is now, comparatively, as bare as a mole-hill.

To the westward, adjoining the house, lay the common or fell, which extended some few miles in length, and was of various breadths. It was mostly fine greensward or pasturage, broken or divided, indeed, with clumps of 'blossom'd whins', foxglove, fern, and some junipers, and with heather in profusion, sufficient to scent the whole air. Near the burns, which guttered its sides, were to be seen the remains of old oaks, hollowed out by Time, with alders, willows, and birch, which were often to be met with in the same state; and these seemed to me to point out the length of time that these domains had belonged to no one. On this common—the poor man's heritage for ages past, where he kept a few sheep, or a Kyloe cow, perhaps a flock of geese, and mostly a stock of bee-hives—it was with infinite pleasure that I long beheld the beautiful wild scenery which was there exhibited, and it is with the opposite feelings of regret that I now find all swept away. Here and there on this common were to be seen the cottage, or rather hovel, of some labouring man, built at his own expense, and mostly with his own hands; and to this he always added a garth and a garden, upon which great pains and labour were bestowed to make both productive; and for this purpose not a bit of manure was suffered to be wasted away on the 'lonnings' or public roads. These various concerns excited the attention and industry of the hardy occupants, which enabled them to prosper, and made them despise being ever numbered with the parish poor.

These men, whose children were neither pampered nor spoiled, might truly be called—

'A bold peasantry, their country's pride';

and to this day I think I see their broad shoulders and their hardy sun-burnt looks, which altogether bespoke the vigour of their constitutions.

These cottagers (at least those of them I knew) were of an honest and independent character, while at the same time they held the neighbouring gentry in the greatest estimation and respect; and these, again, in return, did not overlook them, but were interested in knowing that they were happy and well. Most of these poor men, from their having little intercourse with the world, were in all their actions and behaviour truly original; and, except reading the Bible, local histories, and old ballads, their knowledge was generally limited. And yet one of these—'Will Bewick'—from being much struck with my performances, which he called pictures, became exceedingly kind to me, and was the first person from whom I gathered a sort of general knowledge of astronomy and of the magnitude of the universe. He had, the year through, noticed the appearances of the stars and the planets, and would discourse largely on the subject. I think I see him yet, sitting on a mound, or seat, by the hedge of his garden, regardless of the cold, and intent upon viewing the heavenly bodies; pointing to them with his large hands, and eagerly imparting his knowledge to me with a strong voice such as one now seldom hears. I well remember being much struck with his appearance—his stern-looking brows, high cheek bones, quick eye, and longish visage; and at his resolution (upon another occasion) when he determined upon risking his own life to save that of another man. The latter, in the employ of my father, while at work as a pitman, had lost his way in the coal workings, and was missing for perhaps a day or two (my father being from home), when our old neighbour, just described, who was also a pitman and knew the workings, equipped himself with everything he thought necessary for so hazardous an undertaking; and, when he was about to go down the pit shaft, I felt much distressed at seeing my mother trembling in great agitation of mind for his safety and that of his lost associate. After traversing through the old workings of the colliery for a long time—so long, indeed, that it was feared he had also lost himself, he found the man alive, when, with his well-known thundering voice, he called from the bottom of the shaft,'All's well', to the inexpressible joy of all who crowded the pit's mouth.

Another of our fell-side neighbours, Anthony Liddell, was a man of a very singular character, and was noticed as such by the whole neighbourhood; but a full account of him would far exceed the bounds I wish to set to my narrative. He might, indeed, be called the 'village Hampden'. The whole cast of his character was formed by the Bible, which he had read with attention, through and through. Acts of Parliament which appeared to him to clash with the laws laid down in it, as the Word of God, he treated with contempt. He maintained that the fowls of the air and the fish of the sea were free for all men; consequently, game laws, or laws to protect the fisheries, had no weight with him. He would not, indeed, take a salmon out of the locks on any account, but what he could catch with his 'click-hook', in the river, he deemed his own. As to what he could do in shooting game, he was so inexpert, that he afforded to sportsmen many a hearty laugh at his awkwardness; for he could shoot none till he fixed a hay-fork in the ground to rest his piece upon. Indeed, the very birds themselves might, by a stretch of imagination, be supposed also to laugh at him; but his deficiencies did not deter him from traversing over the countryside as eagerly as other

E 29

sportsmen, notwithstanding his want of success. Whatever he did was always done in open day; for, as he feared no man, he scorned to skulk or to do anything by stealth. The gaol had no terrors for him, for he lived better there than he did at home; and on one occasion of his being confined when he returned home he expressed his surprise to his neighbours, that all the time 'he had not had a single hand's turn to do', and exulted not a little that the opportunity had thus been given him of again reading the Bible through. He was a great reader of history, especially those parts where wars and battles were described; and, in any meetings with his neighbours, he took the lead in discourses founded on knowledge of that kind. After the Bible, 'Josephus' was his favourite author, next the 'Holy Wars'—these and 'Bishop Taylor's Sermons' composed his whole library; and his memory enabled him nearly to repeat whatever he had read. His deportment and behaviour were generally the reverse of anything like sauciness; but, except in ability and acquirements—which, indeed, commanded his respect—he treated all men as equals. When full-dressed, he wore a rusty black coat. In other respects he was like no other person. In what king's reign his hat had been made was only to be guessed at, but the flipes* of it were very large. His wig was of the large curled kind, such as was worn about the period of the revolution.† His waistcoat, or doublet, was made of the skin of some animal. His buckskin breeches were black and glossy with long wear, and of the same antiquated fashion as the rest of his apparel. Thus equipt, and with his fierce look, he made a curious figure when taken before the justices of the peace; and this, together with his always —when summoned before them—undauntedly pleading his own cause, often afforded them so much amusement

* [fold; flap. Scotland and north of England.]
† [of 1688.]

that it was difficult for them to keep their gravity. Others of them of a more grave deportment made use of threats to make him behave more respectfully. These he never failed to show that he despised, and on one occasion of this kind, he told the Justice that 'he was not a bit flaid of him'—that there was 'nobbit yen place that he was flaid of and that was Hell, and he could not send him there'. After this quarrel he was ordered out of court. He waited below in expectation of the Justice's following him to have the matter settled by a fight, and desired a gentleman to tell the Justice that he waited for him for that purpose. When he was told he had behaved insolently to him—'Oh sir', said he (spitting into his hands) 'tell him to come here—he does not know what a fellow aw is (I am).'

Thomas Forster was a man of a different character from the last, but singular enough in his way. He was distinguished for his frugality and industry, and always showed a wish to be looked upon in a respectable light. He used to call at our house on a Sunday afternoon, for the purpose of having a bit of chat with my father and mother. He took a liking to me, and would observe that, though I was mischievous enough, yet he never could find that I was 'parrentory'—that is, impudent or saucy with anyone. Besides this part of the good opinion he had formed, he must have had confidence as to my keeping any secrets he might impart to me. He kept a few sheep on the fell; but his secret and main business there was looking after his bees. He had a great number of hives placed in very hidden and curious situations. Some of them were concealed under the boundary hedge of the common, and were surrounded by a great extent of whin bushes. Other hives were sheltered under the branches of old thorns, and almost covered or overhung by brambles, woodbine, and hip briars, which, when in blossom, looked beautifully picturesque, while at the same time they served to keep the eye from

31

viewing the treasures thus concealed beneath. Others, again, were placed in the midst of a 'whin rush'—that is, a great extent of old whins, the stems of which were about the thickness of a man's arm. The entrance to these last was always by a 'smout hole', or small opening, through which we crept on hands and knees to the hives, and which, on leaving, was stopped up by a bushy-topped whin. By way of taking off the attention of the 'over-inquisitive' as to his stock of honey, he kept hives in his garden at home, and sold the produce of these to his neighbours; but the greater part of his stock was sold at distant parts of the country. In this way, and by his industry and good management, he became what was accounted very rich; and, as prosperity excites envy, some people, in a kind of derision (his mother being a midwife), called him 'Tom Howdy'.

I might swell the list of suchlike characters (among the unnoticed poor) as those I have described, but it would perhaps be tedious, although, I think it is to be regretted that they are not better known to some of the unthinking *Great*; as it might serve to take off the hauteur, which is too often shown towards them.

Another of these uncultivated, singular characters, which exhibit human nature left to the guidance of its uncontrolled will, but which, sometimes, may be found—from the force of innate natural pride—to soar above every meanness, was John Chapman. This man, though clothed in rags, was noticed for his honour and integrity; and his word was considered to be as good as a thousand pounds bond. He was one of my father's workmen—either as a pitman, a labourer, or a sinker—and was of so strong a constitution that he thought it no hardship, on a cold, frosty morning, to be let down to the bottom of a sinking pit, where he was to be up to the middle, or perhaps to the breast, in water, which he was to lave into buckets, to be

32

drawn up to the top. He endured the labour of every job he undertook without grumbling or thinking it hard. His living was of the poorest kind. Bread, potatoes, and oatmeal, was the only provender he kept by him; and with milk or water he finished his repasts. When, by this mode of living, he had saved the overplus money of his wages for a month or six weeks, he then posted off to Newcastle to spend it in beer; and this he called 'lowsening his skin'. I was at this time located in Newcastle, and when the misguided man had spent all his money, he commonly borrowed two shillings of me to set him home again. In this irrational way of life he continued for many years. On one occasion, when changing his beer house, and taking up his quarters in another, he had made no stipulation with his new landlord as to the place where he was to sleep at night; and, judging from his ragged appearance, he was thought unfit to be trusted as an inmate without inquiry being made into his character. I was, therefore, applied to by the landlord, whom I satisfied by assuring him that, notwithstanding the outward appearance of his singular-looking guest, he might be trusted safely even with untold gold. I further told him that the man who could sleep upon the fallen leaves in a wood wanted no bed in his house better than a wooden seat, which would be as comfortable a bed as he would wish for. Matters being now perfectly settled, he was permitted, during his rambles, to make this house his home. He had been but a short time in this asylum until he got a pretty numerous acquaintance amongst the tradesmen who frequented the house, to whom his singularity, his droll and witty stories, and his songs, afforded great entertainment. Old age, however, overtook him at last, and he was then obliged to seek parish relief. On this occasion, a neighbouring laird persuaded him that his settlement* was upon Eltringham, and prevailed on him to swear

* [The Poor Law liability in respect of an applicant for relief.]

to it. When he called upon the farmers there for his pittance, and they convinced him that he had sworn to what was false, he was much shocked, and never called upon them again for his pay. On being asked why he had not done so, he said, 'I would sooner have my hand cut off, or be found dead on the highway through want, than claim or receive money to which I am not justly entitled'. After this he wandered away from Eltringham, and took up his abode in the glass-house at Bill Quay, where he did any little jobs in his power, and at the same time made himself very agreeable and often very entertaining to the workmen, who long remembered 'Johnny Chapman'. From this place he set off on a visit to a friend, at some distance, when he was rather unwell, and not very able to undertake the journey, and was found dead on the road between Morpeth and Newcastle.

Before taking leave of these hardy inhabitants of the fells and wastes, whose cottages were surrounded with whins and heather, I must observe that they always appeared to me, notwithstanding their apparent poverty, to enjoy health and happiness in a degree surpassing that of most other men. Their daily fare was coarse bread, potatoes, oatmeal porridge, and milk, only varied by their boiling the pot with animal food, cabbage, or other succulent vegetables, and broth, on Sundays. When tired at night with labour, having few cares to perplex them, they lay down and slept soundly, and arose refreshed from their hard beds early in the morning. I have always felt much pleasure in revisiting them, and, over a tankard of ale, in listening to their discourse. It was chiefly upon local biography, in which they sometimes traced the pedigree of their neighbours a long way back. When good eating became the subject of their discourse, in telling what they liked, one man would declare that 'over all fruit that grew he liked potatoes and cabbage the best', while another would press upon the audience the deliciousness of potatoes and onion sauce, and in the warmth of his loyalty would wish that the King could but know how good a dish this was, in which case he would never want it for his supper. With the aged men I felt much amused. From the avidity with which they gathered news, they seemed to live upon it. Several of them met every day at the lodge, or earth-built hovel, close by my father's pit, for the purpose of being gratified in this way. The carts and wains came in all directions, and many of them from a great distance, for coals, the drivers of which imparted to them all they knew of what was going on in their several neighbourhoods. In this kind of treat I often partook with them when I was gin driver, by slipping in among them between the drawing up of each cart of coals to the bank. The information thus obtained was then speedily given in detail at the smith's shop at Mickley, whence it was spread over the neighbouring country. One of these old men, John Newton (the laird of the Neuk), almost every morning, while I was young, met me and my schoolfellows at or near the Haly Well (Holy Well) as we were going to Mickley School, and he seldom passed me without clapping my head, accompanied with some good wishes. Many years after this, while I lived at the Forth, Newcastle, I met a little boy, one morning coming to school there, when I clapped his head, and hoped he was a good boy. I had not long passed him, till I was rather struck with the coincident recollection of his grandfather's grandfather (above named) so long before having passed me in the same way.

To these I must add another description of men scattered about the neighbourhood, with whose histories and narratives I at that time felt greatly interested. Their minute account of the battles they had been engaged in, with the hardships they had endured, and their hairbreadth escapes, told with so much enthusiasm and exultation, imparted the same kind of feeling to me. This was long before I had reasoned myself into a detestation of war, its cruelty, its horrors, and the superlative wickedness of the authors of it. I had not pictured to my mind the thousands and tens of thousands of men in their prime being pitted against a like number of others towards whom they could have no enmity —to murder each other!!—for what: It is foreign to my purpose to enlarge upon this subject; I must leave that to others; and there is an abundant scope to dilate upon, and to depicture, the horrors of war in their true colours. The old soldiers, above alluded to, were mostly the descendants of the Borderers, whose propensity for war might, perhaps, be innate. I think however that the breed is thinned, from the numbers that have been killed off in our wars. One of these—a near relative—would describe how he had had his knapsack, as well as his coat laps and the cocks of his hat, shot through and through, and yet had escaped unhurt. Others of them would give similar descriptive accounts; and, when a party of them met over their ale, it is not easy to depicture the warmth with which they greeted each other, and prided themselves on the battles they had won. One of these, during a walk, in which I fell in with him, from Newcastle to Ovingham, described the minute parti- culars of the battle of Minden; and how, in the absence of Lord Sackville, they shook hands the whole length of the line, vowing to stand by each other without flinching. This tall, stout man, John Cowie, though old, appeared to be in all the vigour of youth. He lived at Ovington.* His associate, Ben Garlick, of Prudhoe,† appeared as if his constitution had been broken down. They had served in a corps called Napier's Grenadiers. Cowie appeared occa- sionally in his old military coat, etc. After he died, this

* [About two miles west of Ovingham.]
† [Prudhoe, with its ruined castle (once a Percy stronghold), stands high on the south bank of the Tyne, facing Ovingham.]

coat, which had been shot at at Minden and elsewhere, was at last hung up on a stake on the corn rigs as a scarecrow.

The ferocious people from whom, as I have intimated, the above individuals were probably descended, bore nearly the same names on both sides of the Border; their character seemed to have been distinct from both their English and Scottish neighbours; and war and rapine had long been their almost constant employment. Many of these—the retainers of the chieftains of old, whose feet were swift to shed blood—were called by names which were descriptive of their characters and persons, and which were mostly continued by their offspring. These consisted of a great variety of names of cunning or ferocious birds and beasts, as well as some others, the meaning of which is now unknown. There were among them the Hawk, Glead, Falcon, Fox, Wolf, Bloodhound, Greyhound, Raven, Crow, Gorfoot, Crowfoot, etc., etc.

The farmers of the neighbourhood, at the early period which I have been describing, always appeared to me to be not of so intelligent a cast as the poor labouring men. Their minds being more exclusively occupied with the management of their farms, they read but little. They were mostly of a kind and hospitable disposition, and well-intentioned, plain, plodding men, who went jogging on in their several occupations as their fathers had done before them.

The next advance in society were the Lairds, who lived upon their own lands. I have always, through life, been of opinion that there is no business of any kind that can be compared to that of a man who farms his own land. It appears to me that every earthly pleasure, with health, is within his reach. But numbers of these men were grossly ignorant, and in exact proportion to that ignorance they were sure to be offensively proud. This led them to attempt appearing above their station, which hastened them on to their ruin; but, indeed, this disposition and this kind of conduct invariably leads to such results. There were many of these lairds on Tyneside; as well as many who held their lands on the tenure of 'suit and service', and were nearly on the same level as the lairds. Some of the latter lost their lands (not fairly I think) in a way they could not help; many of the former, by their misdirected pride and folly, were driven into towns, to slide away into nothingness, and to sink into oblivion, while their 'ha' houses' (halls), that ought to have remained in their families from generation to generation, have mouldered away. I have always felt extremely grieved to see the ancient mansions of many of the country gentlemen, from somewhat similar causes, meet with a similar fate. The gentry should, in an especial manner, prove by their conduct that they are guarded against showing any symptom of foolish pride, at the same time that they soar above every meanness, and that their conduct is guided by truth, integrity, and patriotism. If they wish the people to partake with them in these good qualities, they must set them the example, without which no real respect can ever be paid to them. Gentlemen ought never to forget the respectable station they hold in society, and that they are the natural guardians of public morals, and may with propriety be considered as the head and the heart of the country, while 'a bold peasantry' are, in truth, the arms, the sinews, and the strength of the same; but when these last are degraded, they soon become dispirited and mean, and often dishonest and useless.

I think the late Duke of Northumberland must have had an eye to raising the character of the peasantry when he granted them small portions of land at a reasonable rate. If so, in my way of judging, he was an honour to the peerage, and set an example worthy of himself and worthy of imitation. By going a step further, and planting healthy, strong, men and women on these spots, his patriotism would have been crowned with immortality; for I cannot help thinking that, if the same pains were taken in breeding mankind that gentlemen have bestowed upon the breeding of horses and dogs, human nature might, as it were, be new modelled, hereditary diseases banished, and such a race might people the country as we can form no conception of. Instead of a nation of mongrels, there would in time appear a nation of 'Admirable Crichtons'. If the lands commonly attached to townships had been continued as such, and let in small portions to mechanics and labourers (as the late Duke let them), instead of dividing them by Act of Parliament among those who already had too much, the good effects to the community at large would have been soon felt; and, in addition to this, if savings banks and benefit societies were encouraged by every possible means, there would be little occasion for poor laws except as a provision for helpless children, and the lame and the blind. By such means as these, perhaps, this national evil might be done away. All men ought to provide for the necessities of old age, and be made sensible of the manly pleasure of being independent. It is degrading, and in most cases disgraceful, to those who look to parish assistance after a life spent in laziness and mismanagement.

I must not omit mentioning a circumstance that happened to Eltringham while I was a boy. It was to have been called 'Little Birmingham', but this was not accomplished. In 17—, a person of the name of Laidler, who was said to have amassed a large fortune in London, came to the North, and established the Iron Works at Busy Cottage, near Newcastle; and, on his taking a view of Tyneside, he fixed upon Eltringham as a place at which he could carry on works to a much greater extent. He set about this business in great haste. All kinds of workmen were gathered together for the purpose of speedily accomplishing what he had in view; and, while some of them were busy in making the mills and machinery, others were digging a mill-race of about a quarter of a mile in length. But lo! when this was done—not being permitted to encroach on the bed of the river—it was found they had not much more than a foot of waterfall; and, as the sides of the mill-race were cut perpendicularly, about two yards deep, through the dark fine soil, the first great flood of the Tyne nearly levelled and filled it up. The people in and about the place, including my father, who had got licences to sell ale, etc., were obliged to decline, and the sign of my father's house—the Seven Stars—which hung up between the two ash trees, was taken down. The projector made our house his home while the works were going on, and the men were paid their wages there. All was as suddenly sold off as it was begun, and my father came to some loss after all the trouble and turmoil he had been put to.

J Bewick

Joe Liddell

CHAPTER IV

BEING now nearly fourteen years of age, and a stout boy, it was thought time to set me off to business; and my father and mother had long been planning and consulting, and were greatly at a loss what it would be best to fix upon. Any place where I could see pictures, or where I thought I could have an opportunity of drawing them, was such only as I could think of. A Newcastle bookseller, whose windows were filled with prints, had applied to Mr Gregson for a boy; and, when I was asked if I would like to go to him, I readily expressed my hearty consent; but, upon my father making enquiry respecting him, he was given to understand that he bore a very bad character; so that business was at an end. The same year—1767—during the summer, William Beilby* and his brother Ralph took a ride to Bywell, to see their intimate acquaintance, Mrs Simons, who was my godmother, and the widow of the late vicar there. She gave them a most flattering account of me; so much so, that they, along with her and her

* [Introduction, pp. xix.]

daughter (afterwards Mrs Hymers), set off that same afternoon to Cherryburn to visit us, and to drink tea. When the Newcastle visitors had given an account of their paintings, enamellings, drawings, and engravings, with which I felt much pleased, I was asked which of them I should like to be bound to; and, liking the look and deportment of Ralph the best, I gave the preference to him. Matters bearing upon this business were slightly talked over, and my grandmother having left me twenty pounds for an apprentice fee, it was not long till a good understanding between parties took place, and I soon afterwards went to R. Beilby upon trial.

The first of October was the day fixed upon for the binding. The eventful day arrived at last, and a most grievous one it was to me. I liked my master; I liked the business; but to part from the country, and to leave all its beauties behind me, with which I had been all my life charmed in an extreme degree—and in a way I cannot describe—I can only say my heart was like to break; and, as we passed away, I inwardly bade farewell to the whinny wilds, to Mickley bank, to the Stob-cross hill, to the water-banks, the woods, and to particular trees, and even to the large hollow old elm, which had lain perhaps for centuries past, on the haugh near the ford we were about to pass, and which had sheltered the salmon fishers, while at work there, from many a bitter blast. We called upon my much esteemed schoolfellow, Kit Gregson, at Ovingham, where he and his father were waiting to accompany us to Newcastle—all on the same errand—(we were both bound on that day). While we were condoling—comforting each other—I know not what to call it—at the parsonage gates, many of the old neighbours assembled at the churchyard wall, to see us set off, and to express their good wishes; and, amongst the rest, was a good sensible old woman of the village, named Betty Kell, who gave us her blessing, and each a penny for good luck. This being done, our horses were mounted, and we commenced our journey. The parties kept at a little distance from each other. I suppose our late preceptor was lecturing his son, and my father was equally busied in the same way with me. He had always set me the example and taken every opportunity of showing how much he detested meanness, and of drawing forth every particle of pride within me, for the purpose of directing it in the right way. He continued a long while on subjects of this kind, and on the importance and inestimable value of honour and honesty; and he urgently pressed upon me to do my duty to my master, in faithfully and obediently fulfilling all his commands, to be beforehand in meeting his wishes, and, in particular, to be always upon my guard against listening to the insinuations and the wicked advice of worthless persons, who I would find ever ready to poison my ear against him. He next turned his discourse on another topic—new to me from him—of great importance—religion—and pressed this also upon me in a way I did not forget. He begged I would never omit, morning and evening, addressing myself to my Maker, and said that if I ceased to do so, then he believed every evil would follow. I was greatly surprised to hear him dwell on this subject; for I think it was the first time. He used, indeed, to go to church; but I do not recollect his ever commenting upon the sermons he heard there, further than that, the good man's discourse from the pulpit seemed to him to be wasted upon the majority of his congregation, and of his calling some of them 'holy professors'. My mother, who was of a religious turn, had, indeed, all her life, endeavoured to make me so too; but, as I did not clearly understand her well-intended lectures, they made little impression. My father's pithy illustrations, as before hinted at, were much more forcibly and clearly made out: I understood them well, and they operated powerfully upon me. I have often reflected since upon the very high importance, and the necessity, of instilling this species of education into the minds of youth; for, were pains taken to draw forth the pride naturally implanted in their minds for the wisest and best purposes, if properly directed, it would exalt human nature, and be of the utmost importance to individuals and to society. It is the want of this education, and the want of industry, that occasions and spreads misery over the land. How can I doubt that, if my father had been a thief, I would have been one also, or, if a highwayman or robber, as expert as himself. In my opinion, there are two descriptions of persons who ought to forbear, or be prevented, from marrying—viz., those of a base, wicked, and dishonest character, and those who have broken down their constitutions and debased both mind and body by dissipation. The latter entail misery upon their innocent offspring: the children of the former, by the bad example shown to them, become a curse to the community in which they live.

When we arrived at the Cock Inn, Newcastle, the documents were soon made ready to bind my companion and myself. He was bound to Messrs Doughty and Wiggins, chemists and druggists; but Mr Beilby (perhaps from his having heard some unfavourable account of me) and my father not readily agreeing upon the exact terms of my servitude, some fears were entertained that the business between us might be broken off. On this occasion my preceptor interfered very ardently, spoke warmly in my praise, and dwelt forcibly, in particular (notwithstanding my wild, boyish behaviour at school), upon my never being saucy or sulky, nor in the least indulging in anything like revenge. In this business, Mr Gregson was ably seconded by his relation and my kind friend, Mr Joseph Langstaff, of Newcastle, who was also acquainted with my new master; and so the business of binding was settled at last.

44

My new master, who, I believe, had laid down plans for the regulation of his own conduct, began with me upon a system of rigid discipline, from which he never varied or relaxed, and it was not long before I gave occasion to his putting it in force. Having walked out on a Sunday afternoon to see the environs of the town, the first place that attracted my attention was 'King Jamie's Well'. There I fell in with bad company, consisting of three low blackguard 'prentice lads, from the Close.* Having no wish to have anything to say to them, I endeavoured to shun their company; but they, seeing me in a strange and perhaps somewhat clownish dress, followed and insulted me; and this they persisted in till I could bear it no longer, when, turning upon one of the sauciest of them, I presently levelled him, and was about serving the second in the same way, when they all three fell upon me and showed no mercy, so that, in the end, I went home to my master's house with a scratched face and black eyes. This was an abominable sight to the family, which no excuse could palliate. After this, I was obliged to attend my master to church twice a day, every Sunday, and, at night, to read the Bible, or some other good book, to old Mrs Beilby and her daughter, or others of the family; and this continued during the time of the term I boarded in the house with them.

The father of Mr Beilby followed the business of a goldsmith and jeweller in Durham, where he was greatly respected. He had taken care to give all his family a good education. His eldest son, Richard, had served his apprenticeship to a diesinker, or seal engraver, in Birmingham. His second son, William, had learned enamelling and painting in the same place. The former of these had taught my master seal-cutting, and the latter taught his brother Thomas and sister Mary enamelling and painting; and, in

* [A part of the old city, lying south-west of the Castle and very near the river-side.]

45

this way, this most industrious and respectable family lived together and maintained themselves. But, prior to this state of things, while the family were more dependent upon the industry of their father, he had failed in business, left Durham, and begun business in Gateshead, where he and his eldest son Richard died.

I have been informed that the family had to struggle with great difficulties about this period, and that, by way of helping to get through them, their mother taught a school in Gateshead. But this state of things could not have lasted long; for the industry, ingenuity, and united energies of the family must soon have enabled them to soar above every obstacle. My master had wrought as a jeweller with his father before he went to his brother Richard to learn seal-cutting, which was only for a very short time before his death. He had also assisted his brother and sister in their constant employment of enamel painting upon glass. At this time a circumstance happened which made an opening for my future master to get forward in busines unopposed by anyone. An engraver of the name of Jameson, who had the whole stroke of the business in Newcastle, having been detected in committing a forgery upon the old bank, he was tried for the crime. His life was saved by the perjury of a Mrs Gray, who was, I believe, transported for it, and Jameson left the town.

For some time after I entered the business, I was employed in copying 'Copeland's Ornaments', and this was the only kind of drawing upon which I ever had a lesson given to me from anyone. I was never a pupil to any drawing master, and had not even a lesson from William Beilby, or his brother Thomas, who, along with their other profession, were also drawing masters.* In the later years of my apprenticeship, my master kept me so fully em-

* [In Whitehead's first *Newcastle Directory* of 1778 'William Beilby, Northumberland Street,' appears as the town's sole drawing master.]

46

ployed that I never had an opportunity for such a purpose, at which I felt much grieved and disappointed. The first jobs I was put to do was blocking-out the wood about the lines on the diagrams (which my master finished) for the 'Ladies Diary', on which he was employed by Charles Hutton, and etching sword blades for William and Nicholas Oley, sword manufacturers, etc., at Shotley Bridge. It was not long till the diagrams were wholly put into my hands to finish. After these, I was kept closely employed upon a variety of other jobs; for such was the industry of my master that he refused nothing, coarse or fine. He undertook everything, which he did in the best way he could. He fitted-up and tempered his own tools, and adapted them to every purpose, and taught me to do the same. This readiness brought him in an overflow of work, and the work-place was filled with the coarsest kind of steel stamps, pipe moulds, bottle moulds, brass clock faces, door plates, coffin plates, bookbinders' letters and stamps, steel, silver, and gold seals, mourning rings, etc. He also undertook the engraving of arms, crests, and cyphers, on silver, and every kind of job from the silversmiths; also engraving bills of exchange, bank-notes, invoices, account heads, and cards. These last he executed as well as did most of the engravers of the time; but what he excelled in was ornamental silver engraving. In this, as far as I am able to judge, he was one of the best in the kingdom; and, I think, upon the whole, he might be called an ingenious, self-taught artist. The higher department of engraving, such as landscape or historical plates, I dare say, was hardly ever thought of by my master; at least not till I was nearly out of my apprenticeship, when he took it into his head to leave me in charge of the business at home, and to go to London for the purpose of taking lessons in etching and engraving large copper plates. There was, however, little or no employment in this way in Newcastle, and he had no opportunity of becoming clever at it; so he kept labouring on with such work as before named, in which I aided him with all my might. I think he was the best master in the world for teaching boys, for he obliged them to put their hands to every variety of work. Every job, coarse or fine, either in cutting or engraving, I did as well as I could, cheerfully; but the business of polishing copper plates, and hardening and polishing steel seals, was always irksome to me. I had wrought at such as this a long time, and at the coarser kind of engraving (such as I have noticed before), till my hands had become as hard and enlarged as those of a blacksmith. I, however, in due time, had a greater share of better and nicer work given me to execute; such as the outside and inside mottoes on rings, and sometimes arms and crests on silver, and seals of various kinds, for which I made all the new steel punches and letters. We had a great deal of seal-cutting, in which my master was accounted clever, and in this I did my utmost to surpass him.

While we were going on in this way, we were occasionally applied to by printers to execute wood-cuts for them. In this branch my master was very defective. What he did was wretched. He did not like such jobs; on which account they were given to me; and the opportunity this afforded of drawing the designs on the wood was highly gratifying to me. It happened that one of these—a cut of the 'George and Dragon' for a bar bill—attracted so much notice, and had so many praises bestowed upon it, that this kind of work greatly increased, and orders were received for cuts for children's books; chiefly for Thomas Saint, printer, Newcastle, and successor of John White, who had rendered himself famous for his numerous publications of histories and old ballads. With the singing of the latter, the streets of Newcastle were long greatly enlivened; and, on market days, visitors, as well as the town's people, were often highly gratified with it. What a cheerful, lively time this appeared to me and many others! This state of things, however, changed when public matters cast a surly gloom over the character of the whole country; and these singing days, instead of being regulated by the magistrates, were, in their wisdom, totally put an end to.

My time now became greatly taken up with designing and cutting a set of wood blocks for the 'Story-Teller', 'Gay's Fables', and 'Select Fables', together with cuts of a similar kind, for other printers. Some of the Fable cuts were thought so well of by my master that he, in my name, sent impressions of a few of them to be laid before the Society for the Encouragement of Arts, etc., and I obtained a premium. This I received shortly after I was out of my apprenticeship, and it was left to my choice whether I would have it in a gold medal, or money (seven guineas). I preferred the latter; and I never in my life felt greater pleasure than in presenting it to my mother. On this occasion, amongst the several congratulations of kind neighbours, those of Mr Gregson, my old master, stood preeminent. He flew from Ovingham, where the news first arrived, over to Eltringham, to congratulate my father and mother; and the feelings and overflowings of his heart can be better imagined than described.

CHAPTER V

DURING the time I was an inmate in my master's house, along with his mother, brothers, and sister, I attended his brother's horse, and made myself as useful to the family as I could. At that time I had no acquaintances—at least none to be very intimate with. I needed none. I wandered in the fields, and on the Town Moor, alone, and amused myself with my own thoughts. When the time arrived that I was to cater for myself upon four shillings and sixpence per week, and afterwards upon five shillings a week, I went to lodge with my aunt Blackett, in the Pudding Chare, who, being the widow of a freeman,* kept cows upon the Moor, and I was abundantly supplied with milk, which was the chief thing I lived upon.

At Mrs Blackett's I became acquainted with Gilbert Gray, bookbinder; and this singular and worthy man was

---

* Thomas Blackett, silversmith. He was one of my godfathers, and had been foreman to the late John Langlands, by whom he was much noticed as a man of a most intrepid spirit. He was remarkable for his honour, honesty and punctuality.

perhaps the most invaluable acquaintance and friend I ever met with. His moral lectures and advice to me formed a most important succedaneum to those imparted by my parents. His wise remarks, his detestation of vice, his industry, and his temperance, crowned with a most lively and cheerful disposition, altogether made him appear to me as one of the best of characters. In his workshop I often spent my winter evenings. This was also the case with a number of young men, who might be considered as his pupils; many of whom, I have no doubt, he directed into the paths of truth and integrity, and who revered his memory through life. He rose early to work, lay down when he felt weary, and rose again when refreshed, His diet was of the simplest kind; and he ate when hungry, and drank when dry, without paying regard to meal times. By steadily pursuing this mode of life, he was enabled to accumulate sums of money from ten to thirty pounds. This enabled him to get books, of an entertaining and moral tendency, printed and circulated at a cheap rate. His great object was, by every possible means, to promote honourable feelings in the minds of youth, and to prepare them for becoming good members of society. I have often discovered that he did not overlook ingenious mechanics, whose misfortunes— perhaps mismanagement—had led them to a lodging in Newgate.* To these he directed his compassionate eye, and for the deserving (in his estimation), he paid their debt, and set them at liberty. He felt hurt at seeing the hands of an ingenious man tied up in prison, where they were of no use either to himself or to the community. This worthy man had been educated for a priest; but he would say to me, 'of a "trouth", Thomas, I did not like their ways'. So he gave up the thoughts of being a priest, and bent his way from Aberdeen to Edinburgh, where he engaged himself to Allan Ramsay, the poet, then a bookseller

* [Newcastle's town gaol and debtors' prison.]

at the latter place, in whose service he was both shopman and bookbinder. From Edinburgh he came to Newcastle, and engaged himself, I believe, to Mr Slack as a bookbinder, and as a faithful and careful inspector of the books printed in that office. Mrs Slack, who was a woman of uncommon abilities and great goodness of heart, did not overlook Gilbert, and he was her right-hand man as long as she lived. He was afterwards employed in the same way to the end of his life under Solomon Hodgson, the successor to Thomas Slack. Gilbert had had a liberal education bestowed upon him. He had read a great deal, and had reflected upon what he had read. This, with his retentive memory, enabled him to be a pleasant and communicative companion, but something of a prejudice against priests stuck by him as long as he lived. I lived in habits of intimacy with him to the end of his life; and, when he died, I, with others of his friends, attended his remains to the grave at the Ballast Hills.

In my attendance at the workshop of Gilbert, I got acquainted with several young men who like myself admired him, but one of the most singular of these was Anthony Taylor, a glass maker. He was a keen admirer of drawings and paintings, but had no opportunity of showing his talents in the arts otherwise than in his paintings and enamellings upon glass, in which way, considering his situation, he was a proficient, and in other respects he was a man of genius and observation. The first interview I had with him was singular enough, and was owing to his having been told that I was the best whistler in England, he himself being remarkable in this way. We soon tried our respective powers and had many a meeting afterwards for that purpose. He expressed himself highly pleased with the loud and powerful way in which I performed my double whistle, and I was equally so at hearing his inimitable shakes and quavers with which his small shrill pipe was graced. I came nearly up to the loud shrill tones of the fife and the deeper ones of the flute, and improved greatly in imitating him, but he could make no alteration or amendment in his manner of performing, and with all his attempts could never whistle louder or deeper than before. We sometimes amused ourselves, turn and turn about, in this way, and both agreed that it was a pity whistling was not more countenanced and encouraged than it was. We kept up an agreeable acquaintance for some years, until he went to the glass works at Leith where he ended his days. While I remained at my aunt Blackett's she would never allow me to whistle in her house, or perform on any instrument; and I could not afterwards find either time or opportunity to gratify my propensity in this way, so I was obliged to make whistling serve for all. I often think that it was scarcely possible for anyone to have a better ear for music than I had, for whatever tunes I heard at Fairs or Hoppings, etc., I could next morning whistle correctly, and not only the tune but the manner of the various performers.

How long I remained with my aunt, I have now forgotten. After I left her house, I went to lodge with Ned Hatfield, whose wife was an excellent cook and market woman, and had long lived in the family of 'Willy Scott', the father of the present Lord Chancellor of England.* She was now chiefly employed in keeping the dancing school of Neil Stewart clean and in good order, and sold oranges and fruit to his pupils. Above the school she had the rooms taken to live in, and to let out to lodgers, and it happened that the young man, John McDonald, Mr Stewart's fiddler, was lodged with her along with me. He was accounted an excellent performer on the violin, and to his performances (the Scottish tunes particularly) I listened with great delight. When Neil Stewart declined, or perhaps died, he was

* [John Scott, Earl of Eldon (1751–1838).]

succeeded in this school by Ivey Gregg, and his fiddler, John Frazier, lodged in the same house with me, and with his music I was also pleased as I had been before. After this my landlord got into a very unfortunate way of doing business. Being a heckler (flax dresser), his brethren prevailed upon him and his wife to permit the tramps—or scamps—in that line to take up their lodgings with them. Here I was introduced, or at least had an opportunity of becoming acquainted with them, and a pretty set they were. Their conduct was wicked in the extreme. The proper effect, however, was produced upon me; for I looked upon their behaviour with the utmost disgust. After poor Ned had for some time been cheated and defrauded by this set, he at length got done with them, and boarded and lodged others of a better cast of character.

Long before the death of my friend Gilbert, I had ceased to have the privilege of reading his books, and what I could save out of my wages only afforded me a scanty supply. I had, however, an opportunity, per favour of my master's servant girl (who admitted me early in the morning into his parlour), of reading through, with great attention, the then new publication of 'Smollett's History of England'; and, for a long time afterwards, I clearly remembered everything of note which it contained. With some of the characters therein depicted, I was greatly pleased, but with others I was shocked and disgusted. They appeared to me like fiends obtruded upon the community, as a curse and a scourge; and yet how surprising it is that some of these can be spoken of, by authors, with complacency. Another source from whence to obtain a supply of books presently fell in my way, through the kindness of William Gray, the son of Gilbert, whose workshop became a place of resort to me and others. He was a bookbinder of some repute, and this led him into employment of a superior cast to that of his father, and his workshop was often filled with works of the best authors. To these, while binding, I had ready access; for which purpose I rose early in the morning; and to him my well-known whistle in the street was the signal for his quickly preparing to get to his work, and I remained with him till my work hour came.

I feel it as a misfortune, that a bias, somehow or other, took place in my mind at this time, which led me deeply into the chaos of what is called religious works; and, for the purpose of getting into a thorough knowledge of all matters of this important kind, I spent much time, and took great pains, to obtain information; but, instead of this, I got myself into a labyrinth—bewildered with dogmas, creeds, and opinions, mostly the fanatical reveries, or the bigoted inventions, of interested or designing men, that seemed to me to be without end; and, after all my pains, I left off in a more unsettled state of mind than when I began. I may be mistaken; but I think, many a well-meaning man has spun out his life, and spent his time, on subjects of this kind in vain. Wagon loads of sermons have been published—some of them, perhaps, good—in order to prove matters (in my opinion) of no importance either to religion or morality. If it be true that everything in perfection is simple, so it must be with religion. There may be many moral and religious duties for man to fulfil in his passage through life; but the rules for doing so are so plain and easily understood that common sense only is necessary for all that is required of us in the performance of them. The beauty and simplicity of the doctrines laid down by the inspired and benevolent Author of the Christian Religion, however they may have been distorted and disfigured, are yet in themselves perfect. They may, indeed, be compared to a mathematical point—a point of perfection—for all men to aim at, but to which none can fully attain. The inspired writings of the prophets of old are also full of simplicity, as well as of indescribable

55

beauty, and may be read and considered with ever-increasing delight. The inspired writers, poets, and moralists, of more modern times, have also laboured most clearly to point out the paths which lead to religion, to virtue, and to happiness. As far as I am able to judge, all we can do is to commune with and reverence and adore the Creator, and to yield with humility and resignation to His will. With the most serious intention of forming a right judgment, all the conclusion I can come to is, that there is only one God and one religion; and I know of no better way of what is called serving God than that of being good to his creatures, and of fulfilling the moral duties, as that of being good sons, brothers, husbands, fathers, neighbours, and members of society.

At this time, I had few that I could call intimate acquaintances. My almost only ones were books, over which I spent my time, mornings and evenings, late and early. This too intense application to books, together with my sedentary employment, and being placed at a very low work bench, took away my healthy appearance, and I put on a more delicate look, and became poorly in health. When my master saw this, he sent for medical aid, and Nathaniel Bailes, surgeon, was consulted. But, before he uttered a word as to my ailment, he took me to his own house, and there he stripped and examined me, and, looking me in the face, told me 'I was as strong as a horse'. He then made up some medicine to cause expectoration. This was all soon done, but not so the lecture he gave my master, whom he addressed in terms which I thought both long and rude. 'What!' said he, 'have you no more sense than to set a growing, country lad to work, doubled up at a low bench, which will inevitably destroy him?' and, in his passion, he cursed poor Beilby for his ignorance or for something worse. From this time the Doctor took a liking to me, and often criticized my work. He also took great pains to direct me how to live and manage myself, under so sedentary an employment; and an intimacy commenced between us which lasted as long as he lived. He urged upon me the necessity of temperance and exercise. I then began to act upon his advice, and to live as he directed, both as to diet and exercise. I had read Lewis Cornaro,* and other books, which treated of temperance; and I greatly valued the advice given in the *Spectator*, which strongly recommended all people to have their days of abstinence. Through life I have experienced the uncommon benefit derived from occasionally pursuing this plan, which always keeps the stomach in proper tone. I regularly pursued my walks, and, whilst thus exercising, my mind was commonly engaged in devising plans for my conduct in life.

For a long time, both in summer and winter, I went to Elswick three times a day, at the expense of a penny each time for bread and milk. I had an hour allowed me for dinner; and, as to my mornings and evenings, I could take a much longer time. A very small matter of animal food, when I missed going to Elswick, was amply sufficient for me; for I think my constitution did not require to be stimulated. By persevering in this system of temperance and exercise, I was astonished to find how much I improved in health, strength, and agility. I thought nothing of leaving Newcastle after I had done work—7 o'clock—on a winter's night, and of setting off to walk to Cherryburn. In this I was stimulated by an ardent desire to visit my parents as often as possible; and the desire continued to act upon me as long as they lived.

In my solitary walks (as before noticed), the first resolution made was that of living within my income; and another of similar import, was that of never getting any-

* [Luigi Cornaro (1467–1566), who lived to the age of ninety-eight, belonged to a Venetian family painted by Titian. Cornaro's *The Sure and Certain Method of Attaining a Long and Healthful Life* enjoyed a great popularity in English translations.]

thing upon trust; but, indeed, my limited income, at this time, led me carefully to observe these rules, and I have never since forgotten them. The train of reflections they brought along with them has also dwelt upon my mind. I could not help observing the inevitable ill consequences which a contrary course (at first entered upon, perhaps, unthinkingly) led thousands into, and the misery it entailed. The more I have thought upon this subject, the more clearly I have seen its importance. Getting into debt is followed by leading people to live beyond their incomes; and this makes all who do so, soon become demoralized and dishonest; and, when the mind has been thus blunted, and degraded, anxiety and trouble must be its attendants, till vice and misery close the scene.

Amongst the acquaintances I made at the workshops of Gilbert and William Gray, was William Bulmer, afterwards rendered famous as the proprietor of the Shakespeare Printing Office, in Cleveland Row, London, who was the first that set the example, and soon led the way, to fine printing in England. He used, while he was an apprentice, to prove the cuts I had executed. In this he was countenanced by his master, John Thompson, who was himself extremely curious and eager to see wood engraving succeed; for at that time the printing of wood-cuts was very imperfectly known.

About this time I commenced a most intimate acquaintance and friendship with Robert Pollard, afterwards an engraver and printseller of eminence in London. He was bound apprentice to John Kirkup, a silversmith in Newcastle; and, from his being frequently sent to our workshop with crests, cyphers, etc., to engrave, he took a great liking to engraving, and was indefatigable in his endeavours to become master of it. In furtherance of this, we spent many of our evenings together at his father's house, which to me was a kind of home. On his master declining business, my young friend was engaged for a term of years to learn engraving with Isaac Taylor, of Holborn, London.

In my frequent visits to the workshops of Gilbert Gray, and to that of his son William, I first fell in with Thomas Spence.* He was one of the warmest philanthropists in the world. The happiness of mankind seemed with him to absorb every other consideration. He was of a cheerful disposition, warm in his attachments to his friends, and in his patriotism to his country; but he was violent against people whom he considered of an opposite character. With such he kept no bounds. For the purpose chiefly of making converts to his opinion 'that property in land is everyone's right', he got a number of young men gathered together, and formed into a debating society, which was held in the evenings in his first schoolroom, in the Broad Garth, Newcastle. One night when his favourite question was to be debated, he reckoned upon me as one of his 'backers'. In this, however, he was mistaken; for, notwithstanding my tacitly assenting in a certain degree to his plan—viz., as to the probability of its succeeding in some uninhabited country or island—I could not at all agree with him in thinking it right to upset the present state of society, by taking from people what is their own, and then launching out upon his speculations. I considered that property ought to be held sacred, and, besides, that the honestly obtaining of it was the great stimulant to industry, which kept all things in order, and society in full health and vigour. The question having been given against him without my having said a word in its defence, he became swollen with indignation, which, after the company was gone, he vented upon me. To reason with him was useless. He began by calling me—from my silence—'a Sir Walter Blackett';† adding,

* [1750–1814.]
† [A Newcastle M.P. at that time, who incurred odium as a political turncoat.]

'If I had been as stout as you are, I would have thrashed you.' 'Indeed!' said I, 'it is a great pity you are not.' 'But,' said he, 'there is another way in which I can do the business, and have at you!' He then produced a pair of cudgels, and to work we fell. He did not know that I was a proficient in cudgel playing, and I soon found that he was very defective. After I had blackened the insides of his thighs and arms, he became quite outrageous and acted very unfairly, which obliged me to give him a severe beating. This, however, did not make a breach between us, for I believe the respect and kindness for each other was mutual.

I cut the steel punches for Spence's types, and my master struck them on the matrices for casting his newly-invented letters of the alphabet, for his 'Spelling and Pronouncing Dictionary'. He published, in London, many curious books in his peculiar way of spelling, and most of them, I believe, on his favourite subject of property in land being everyone's right. However mistaken he might be in his notions on this subject, I am clearly of opinion that his intentions were both sincere and honest.

The next most eccentric individual, and at the same time one of the most worthy characters, I early became acquainted with was George Gray, son of Gilbert, and half-brother of William Gray. He was bound apprentice to a man of the name of Jones, a fruit painter. The latter, who, I believe, was accounted eminent in his profession, lived beyond his income, and departed from Newcastle. George being thus left to himself, commenced in the same way of business, greatly succeeded in it, and then also became eminent as a fruit painter; this he pursued many years, but, from his versatility of disposition, he dipped into almost every art and science, and excelled in many pursuits. He was accounted one of the best botanists and chemists in this part of the country. He was also a geologist, and was fixed upon as a leader or director to a party employed by

Prince Poniatowsky, to take a survey of the various strata of Poland; but George being slovenly in his dress and negligent in his person, felt himself slighted, and left those who put on a more respectable appearance to profit by his superior knowledge, and to do the best they could, and he returned home. Whether it was before or after this time I have forgotten, but he visited North America, and travelled in quest of knowledge pretty far into the interior of that country. On his return he resumed his old employment, in a room never cleaned or swept, and surrounded with models, crucibles, gallipots, brushes, paints, palettes, bottles, jars, retorts, and distils, in such a chaos of confusion as no words can describe. From this *Sanctum Sanctorum*, he corresponded with gentlemen of science in London and other parts. Few men were better liked by private friends—as well for his knowledge as for his honesty, and the genuine simplicity of his manners.

In addition to the various jobs already noticed as keeping my master and myself fully employed, I had others which fell exclusively to my lot to execute; and, amongst these were the mathematical works of Charles Hutton, who frequently came into the room in which I worked to inspect what I was doing. He was always very civil, but seemed to me to be of a grave or shy deportment. He lived in habits of intimacy with my master, and used to write pieces for him to engrave from, particularly for the heads of invoices or bills of parcels; and I remember that he wrote them with an ink, or preparation, which was easily transferred to the copper. This was before his appointment in the royal military academy of Woolwich, in 1773, and long before he had the well-merited title of LL.D added to his respected name. Dr Hutton was that kind of man who never forget old friends; and, some years after, when I was in partnership with my old master, he recommended us to the notice of Dr Horsley, who was commencing his publication of Sir Isaac Newton's works, the execution of the whole of the cuts for which devolved upon me. This transaction took place in 1778.

I continued to take up my abode with Ned Hatfield, and, the spirits being buoyant, everything pleased me. I cannot help noticing the happy time I spent there. I was also entertained with the curious characters who resorted to his house. These were mostly bird-catchers and bird-dealers, to whose narratives respecting their pursuits I listened with some interest while they were enjoying themselves over a tankard of beer. Ned was almost constantly busied in rearing a numerous brood of canaries, which he sold to a bird merchant, who travelled with them at set times to Edinburgh, Glasgow, etc., for sale.

I also, at various periods of the time I remained under Hatfield's roof, got into a knowledge of the misguided ways which too many young fellows pursued; and I watched, and saw the wretched consequences of the kind of life they led. The first of these was a young man from the country of a hale healthy look and also of a good disposition, whose friends had it in their power and intended to enable him to prosper in the world, but he was chopped down in his youthful prime solely by his connecting himself with the bad women of the Town and becoming perfectly tainted by his intercourse with them—two others, his companions, the same as to health, vigour and prospects in life as himself, fell sacrifices in the same way. I felt grieved for them and did all in my power to dissuade them from pursuing such a wretched course of life. For this advice they laughed at me, and called me 'the old man'. It was not very long, however, till two of them sent for me to come and see them on their deathbeds. The die was then cast, and I cannot forget their thanks to me, and the bitterness with which they reproached themselves for not listening to what I had so sincerely recommended. Doctors may palliate the odious disease thus contracted—and some may think in certain stages of it that it can be routed out of the habit—but this I think is doubtful—and under this impression I think that men so patched up ought never to be allowed to marry. Another young fellow (and I am done with them) whose prospects in life were as fair as those I have described, but whose character was of the basest kind, had led a similar course of life and had got the disease patched up and shocking to relate he married—yes, he married—as healthy and beautiful and innocent young woman as could be seen—with a fortune too. Well, in due time there appeared a prospect of his becoming a father. The time came but it is too shocking and disgusting to relate further particulars. Shortly after this, he married another young woman of a similar description as the last, and a similar wretched fate attended her. For a great length of time after this I lost sight of him, but by chance fell in with him again when he accosted me with all the familiarity of an old acquaintance and fellow lodger. I was so overpowered with disgust that a civil return was out of my power to give him. 'So,' said I, 'and is it you? I suppose you think by your having turned Methodist you will rub off your enormous crimes. No, no, you may think that preaching and praying will wipe off the stain, but I think not,' and in the heat of my indignation forgot myself and said, 'if I were God I never would forgive you. What God may do in his infinite mercy I know not.' He died in his prime a short time after this. Such conduct as I have been attempting to describe appears to me to be of the very blackest dye. It is amongst the most cruel and the most shocking of murders. It is to be regretted that the seducer and the seduced cannot by any known law be obliged to live together for life, and, while they live, be allowed to herd only with such as themselves; for they ought to be banished from the society of the modest and virtuous part

63

of the community. I think it a great omission in parents and teachers not to make unguarded youth fully apprized of the risks they run in towns of getting acquainted with the lost and polluted women of this stamp. Nothing can be so sure a guard against this vice as that of making young men see it in its true light—to be disgusted at it. Magistrates, no doubt, have it in their power, in some degree, to lessen this great evil, by preventing abandoned women from appearing in the streets of a town; but I have often felt for magistrates on account of the great and gratuitous trouble they take, and the difficulties they must have to encounter, in their endeavours to keep the wicked within due bounds.

My last fellow-lodgers, before I was out of my apprenticeship, were John Hymers, who had been a sergeant in the Life Guards, and had retired upon his pension, and Whittaker Shadforth, a watch-maker, and also a musician. The latter was of a quite different character from those before noticed, but was wild, enthusiastic, and romantic. When he first came to lodge with us, he had a pale pasty and unhealthy look with his stomach quite out of order— for the amendment of which I began to prescribe for him and for this purpose I ordered him to prepare a quantity of warm camomile tea and then to set himself to work in smoking several pipes of tobacco. The effect produced by these kept him up all night, but gave him a most thorough cleansing and in a little time he appeared with a ruddy complexion and in good health. I next put him upon the same way of living as that I practised myself, and in this he persevered until he became strong and active. Among the many whims and fancies we indulged in, one of them was to learn the manual exercise. The sergeant, who had often laughed at our frolics, very readily agreed to undertake this task, provided we would strictly obey the rules he prescribed to us. This we agreed to. He began with a kind of lecture on the necessity of soldiers being obedient to their officers, and standing like a brick wall without flinching; adding that he would not use his cane upon our backs, but only to put us in mind to be very attentive. This being settled, we were in the mornings to appear before him in 'bare buffs', that is, without our shirts and upper-clothing. This discipline was pursued steadily for some time, notwithstanding the switches he gave us on our bare backs with his rod or cane, which we bore with the utmost *sang froid*. I think the sergeant, notwithstanding the enter-tainment we thus afforded him, began to tire first; for he at last lay in bed while he was giving us our lessons, and at length gave the business up.

From the length of time I had known and noticed Miss Beilby, I had formed a strong attachment to her, but could not make this known to her or to anyone else. I could have married her before I was done with my apprenticeship without any fears on my part, but I felt for her, and pined and fretted at so many bars being in the way of our union. One of the greatest was the supposed contempt in which I was held by the rest of the family, who, I thought, treated me with great hauteur, though I had done everything in my power to oblige them. I had, like a stable boy, waited upon their horse; and had cheerfully done everything they wanted at my hands till one of the brothers grossly affronted me in the business of the stable. This I instantly resented, and refused attendance there any more. Before I was out of my time, Miss Beilby had a paralytic or palsy stroke, which very greatly altered her looks, and rendered her for some time unhappy. Long after this she went with her eldest brother into Fifeshire, where she died.

CHAPTER VI

THE first of October 1774 arrived at last; and, for the first time in my life, I felt myself at liberty. I wrought a few weeks with my old master, and then set off to spend the winter at Cherryburn. There I had plenty of work to do, chiefly from Thomas Angus, printer, Newcastle. I continued there, employed by him and others, till the summer of 1776. This was a time of great enjoyment, for the charms of the country were highly relished by me, and after so long an almost absence from it, gave even that relish a zest which I have not words to describe. I continued to execute wood-cuts and other jobs, but often rambled about among my old neighbours, and became more and more attached to them, as well as to the country.

In the storms of winter, I joined the Nimrods as of old. In spring and summer, my favourite sport of angling was pretty closely followed up. About Christmas, as I had done before when a boy, I went with my father to a distance to collect the money due to him for coals. In these rounds, I

66

had the opportunity of seeing the kindness and hospitality of the people. The countenances of all, both high and low, beamed with cheerfulness; and this was heightened everywhere by the music of old tunes, from the well-known, exhilarating, wild notes of the Northumberland pipes, amidst the buzz occasioned by 'foulpleughs' (morrice or sword dancers) from various parts of the country. This altogether left an impression on my mind which the cares of the world have never effaced from it. The gentry, the farmers, and even the working people, of that day had their Christmas home-brewed ale, made only from malt and hops. This was before the pernicious use of chemical or druggists' compounds was known, or agricultural improvements had quickened the eyes of landlords, banished many small farmers, soured their countenances, and altered for the worse the characters of the larger ones that remained.

Having all my life, at home, at school, and during my apprenticeship, lived under perpetual restraints, when I thus felt myself at liberty, I became, as I suppose, like a bird which had escaped from its cage. Even angling, of which I was so fond, and of which I thought I never could tire, became rather dull when I found I could take as much of it as I pleased. While I was pursuing this sport on a hot day in June, I gave it up; and, laying down my rod awhile, I then tied it up and walked home. Having resolved to see more of the country, I requested my mother to put me up some shirts, etc., and I told her I was going to see my uncle (her brother) in Cumberland. She soon complied with my request, amidst expressions of fear for my safety; showing the natural feelings of a good mother. After sewing three guineas in my breeches waistband, I set off that afternoon, and walked to Haydon Bridge. There I visited my old crony, Thomas Spence, then a teacher in Haydon Bridge school, with whom I was a welcome guest, and stopped two days. Leave of absence from school having been given to him, I rambled with him over the neighbour-hood, and visited everything worth notice. When I departed, he accompanied me on the road nearly to Halt-whistle. After this, I met with little to attract notice except Naworth Castle; and, when I left it, and was proceeding across the country, I lost my way by following paths which led only to holes that had been made by digging peats and turf, and did not reach my uncle's house at Ainstable till late in the evening. I remained at Ainstable about a week, during which time I rambled about the neighbourhood, visited my friends at Kirkoswald and elsewhere, and spent what time I could spare in fishing for trout in the Croglin.

After I had seen Armanthwaite and Penrith, I began to think of moving further abroad; and my cousin having occasion to go to Carlisle, I went with him there, where we parted. I wandered about the old city; and, in the afternoon, looked into the shop of Lowry, the watchmaker, to whom I was known as having been employed, by my master, to engrave many clock faces for him, during my apprenticeship. While I was in his shop, in came a man—a kind of scamp—of the name of Graham, who asked me what road I was going? 'To Scotland,' I replied. 'So am I,' said he; 'and, if you can keep foot with me, I will be glad of your company.' We had no sooner set off, than I found he was a vapouring fop who was very vain of his great prowess as a pedestrian. I could soon see that he wanted to walk me off my foot; but, having been long practised in that way, he found himself mistaken, and long before we reached Longtown he had called in at several public-houses for refreshment, and invited me to do the same. I, however, was not thirsty, and not being used to drink, I sat on the seats at the doors till he came out. He kept on in this way till we reached Langholm, when he surveyed me with an attentive eye, but said nothing.

At Langholm, my landlord, who was a Cumberland man

68

and knew my relatives there, was very kind to me; and, among many other matters concerning them, told me that my cousin who had accompanied me to Carlisle had won nine belts in his wrestling matches in that county. From Langholm, I set off to Hawick and Selkirk and from the latter place, next morning, by Dalkeith, to Edinburgh. I had been, in this short tramp, particularly charmed with the Border scenery; the roads, in places, twined about the bottoms of the hills, which were beautifully green, like velvet, spotted over with white sheep, which grazed on their sides, watched by the peaceful shepherd and his dog. I could not help depicturing in my mind the change which had taken place, and comparing it with the times of old that had passed away, and in inwardly rejoicing at the happy reverse. It is horrid to contemplate the ferocious battles of that day, between men descended from the same stock, and bearing the same names on both sides of the Border, only divided from each other by a river, a rivulet, a burn, or a strip of ground—that they should have been, at the nod of their chieftains, called out to the wild foray by the slogan horn, or the shrill notes of the bugle; that they should have been led to meet and slaughter each other, to manure the ground with their blood, amidst the clash of arms and the thrilling music of the pipes, which helped to excite them on to close their eyes in death. These transactions, which are handed down to their descendants of the present generation in traditionary tales, and kept in remembrance by the songs and tunes of old times, serve now only as food for reflection or amusement.

On entering Edinburgh, having been recommended by Mr Robertson, silversmith, to the landlord of the George Inn,* Bristoport, I halted there; but, being quite un-

* ['As soon as they [Guy Mannering and Dominie Sampson] arrived in Edinburgh, and were established at the George Inn near Bristo Port, then kept by Old Cockburn (I love to be particular) . . .']

acquainted with the customs of living in such places, I knew not what to do, or how to conduct myself. I, however, called for a pint of beer—and I think it was the first I ever called for in my life—when, lo! a good-looking girl, bare-footed and bare-legged, entered with a pewter pot, almost the size of a half leg of a boot. This I thought I could not empty in a week. As I found I could not remain in this place, I sought for another, and luckily fell in with an old Newcastle acquaintance, Mrs Hales, the wife (or widow) of —— Hales, the coachman to Lord Chief Baron Ord; and to her I stated my case, went with her, and felt quite at home in her house. After I had seen as much of 'Auld Reekie' as I could, and been lost in admiration at the grandeur of its situation, and of its old buildings, I next day called upon Hector Gavin, an engraver, in Parliament Close. This kind man—a stranger to me—after a bit of chat about the arts, etc., threw by his tools, and was quite at my service. The warmth of his kindness I never can forget. He took me all over Edinburgh, and gave me a history and explanation of everything he thought worthy of notice. Having parted from him with his best and warmest wishes, I rose early on the next morning and walked to Glasgow. After leaving my bundle at the inn there, to which Mr Robertson had also recommended me, I took a ramble through the city. There I fell in, by chance, with an old acquaintance, Alexander Steedman, a clever cutler, who had lodged with me at Ned Hatfield's, and who I supposed was dead long ago. He was not like me; he could drink plenty; so that I was at no loss what to do at this inn, as I had been in Edinburgh. He called upon me next morning along with a curious and well-informed man, when they showed me everything they thought worthy of notice in Glasgow, which, though a large city, containing many handsome buildings, I was not so charmed with as I had been with Edinburgh.

70

From Glasgow, I set off to Dumbarton; and, on my way, took as good a survey of the country, and whatever was new to me, as I could. My landlord at Dumbarton had seen a deal of the world, either as a soldier or a gentleman's servant, and was very communicative; and I think I spent the next day with him, in walking about and viewing everything that he could think of that might please or entertain me. After leaving him, I wished much to see the printing at the cotton works, and the print fields, as they were called, on the river Leven, near Dumbarton. To these, however, I could not get admission; so I kept passing onward, up the Leven, till Smollett's monument, near the side of it, arrested my attention. There I stopped, for I had read Smollett's works, and almost adored him as an author. On the pedestal of the monument was a long Latin inscription, which I was endeavouring to translate, but was puzzled to make out; having never looked into a Latin book since I had left school; and, for the first time, I felt mortified at not having done so. While I was thus employed up came a 'lish', clever young man, a Highlander, smartly dressed in the garb of his country. He jumped down beside me, and we together made out the translation. When this was done, on learning from me that my sole object was to see Scotland, he pressed me to accompany him to some place or other, the name of which I do not now remember. We, however, walked a long way together on the western side of Loch Lomond, and I know I did not visit Inverary, the seat of Argyle, but stopped with my companion at a grazier's, or farmer's, house, not a long way from it.

Having made up my mind not to visit any town, or put up at any inn, I commenced my 'wild-goose chase', and bent my way, in many a zig-zag direction, through the interior part of the Highlands, by the sides of its lakes and its mountains. The beauty and serenity of the former, and the grandeur or terrific aspect of the latter, I gazed upon with wonder, and with both was charmed to ecstasy. In moving forward, I was often accompanied or directed to some farmer's or grazier's house, by the herds or drovers, whom I fell in with; and, in some of these houses, I took up my abode, and often, by the pressing solicitations of my host or hostess, was prevailed upon to remain with them a day or two. These kind—these hospitable people—I have never forgotten. Often the mistress of the house in these remote places, never having seen any person from England, examined my dress from head to foot, and in English—which, it was easy to discover, had been imperfectly taught her—made many enquiries respecting the country from whence I came; while the herds, with their bare knees, sat listening around, very seldom knowing what we were talking about. These herds, or some of the family, generally set or directed me to the house of some other distant grazier; and I met with the same kind and warm reception throughout my wanderings I had experienced at first. It sometimes happened that, by my having stopped too long on my way, in admiration of the varied prospects I met with, that I was benighted, and was obliged to take myself shelter under some rocky projection or to lay down amongst the heather, till daylight. In my traversings and wanderings, I called in at all the houses on my way, whether situated in the beautiful little valleys, in the glens, or on the sides of heathery hills. In these places it was common to see three houses, one added to another. The first contained a young married couple with their healthy-looking children; the next, or middle one, was occupied by the father and mother, and perhaps the brothers and sisters, of this couple; and, further on, at the end, was the habitation of the old people. These places had always garths and gardens adjoining, with peat stacks and other fuel at hand for the winter; and the whole was enlivened with numbers of ducks, chickens, etc. On my getting some refreshment of whey or milk in such places as these, I always found it difficult to get payment made for anything, as it seemed to give offence; and, when I could get any money slipped into the hands of the children, I was sure to be pursued, and obliged to accept of a pocket full of bannocks and scones.

On one occasion, I was detained all day and all night at a house of this kind, in listening to the tunes of a young man of the family who played well upon the Scottish pipes. I, in turn, whistled several Tyneside tunes to him; so that we could hardly get separated. Before my departure next day, I contrived by stealth to put some money into the hands of the children. I had not got far from the house till I was pursued by a beautiful young woman, who accosted me in 'badish' English, which she must have got off by heart just before she left the house, the purport of which was to urge my acceptance of the usual present. This I wished to refuse; but, with a face and neck blushed with scarlet, she pressed it upon me with such sweetness—while I thought at the same time that she invited me to return—that (I could not help it) I seized her, and smacked her lips. She then sprang away from me, with her bare legs, like a deer, and left me fixed to the spot, not knowing what to do. I was particularly struck with her whole handsome appearance. It was a compound of loveliness, health, and agility. Her hair, I think, had been flaxen or light, but was tanned to a pale brown by being exposed to the sun. This was tied behind with a riband, and dangled down her back; and, as she bounded along, it flowed in the air. I had not seen her while I was in the house, and felt grieved because I could not hope ever to see her more.

After having wandered about in this way for some time longer, during which I uniformly met with the same kind treatment among these unpolluted, unspoiled, honourable, and kind people, I began to think of the long way I had to

73

get over on my return towards home; for, although my money was not greatly diminished among the Highlanders, yet I knew not how much I might want in or near towns, in the more *civilized* districts; so I turned back in a south-easterly direction through the country, where I met, in my various wanderings, the same warm and friendly reception. From that time to this, I have ever felt pleased at the name of Highlander. Were not these people proof against the temptation of a bribe of thirty thousand pounds, held out to them to betray the unfortunate Prince Charles Stuart? Is it not to be regretted that agricultural improvements have taught the landlords, or chieftains, to turn numerous farms into one, and to banish thousands of these hardy descendants of the ancient Britons—this brave race of men to whose forefathers they owed so much—to seek an asylum in foreign climes? In exchange for *men*, they have filled the country with sheep! Property, in every country, should be held sacred, but it should also have its bounds; and, in my opinion, it should be, in a certain degree, held in trust, jointly, for the benefit of its owners, and the good of society. To exercise a right of property beyond this is despotism, the offspring of misplaced aristocratic pride.

I have not noticed that I was sometimes, in passing along, detained at fairs and 'trysts'. These, with their merry-makings, were something like the 'hoppings' and 'feasts' on Tyneside; and the girls had the same ruddy look as the farmers' servants who are put to do field work in Northumberland and Durham. With the Scotch music and dancing, I was very much pleased. They were certainly good dancers, and seemed quite wild, or exhilarated to excess.

I left the Highlands with regret. The last day's journey was a very long one, and a very hungry one; after which I entered Stirling in the night. I told the landlord of the public-house there that I was almost famished, not having stopped at any house on my very long journey to that place; and I begged of him to hasten to get me something to eat. He told me he had nothing left but eggs, as his company had eaten up everything that had been in the house. I did not get my eggs till midnight; for a quarrel, or an affray, happened in the house at the time I ought to have had them. They were brought in to me at last, and were boiled as hard as eggs could be. With them, in my eagerness to eat, I was nearly choked.

I remained about two or three days at Stirling, chiefly on account of my face having been so blistered by the heat of the sun that I thought it best to halt till the effects of it could be removed. My landlord was very kind. He had seen the world; and, when he found that I was an engraver, he expressed his surprise that I had not carried my tools with me; for, if I had done so, he said he had no manner of doubt, with my knowledge of heraldry, etc., that I could have found plenty of employment among the gentry and the lairds, in engraving their arms, crests, and other devices and have earned easily far more than double the money of our Newcastle charges, besides being handed from chieftain to chieftain, and seeing the whole country in a very different way from that which I had, through wildernesses, so wildly pursued. On my way to Edinburgh, by Falkirk, I visited Carron Works,* and passed under the canal, where, for the first time, I saw vessels afloat that had passed over my head. I was also shown the ground where the Battle of Bannockburn was fought.

As soon as I could, I made my way, by Linlithgow, to Edinburgh, and took up my abode again with Mrs Hales. I engaged a passage by sea, in a ship belonging to Whitby, which had to touch at Shields. I attended upon this vessel every tide, late and early, for several days, notwithstanding which I missed my time, and was left behind. In

* [An industrial wonder at that time, the Carron Company's ironworks were established in 1760.]

this emergency, I got on board a Leith sloop, bound for Newcastle, commanded by Captain Kay, then moving from the pier. We had no sooner got down the Firth of Forth, to the open sea, than we met a heavy swell, and presently encountered a violent gale which soon tore our sails to shivers, drove us far out of sight of land, and put our crew in a great bustle and dilemma. In this small vessel, the crew and passengers amounted to twenty-six. For these latter there was no accommodation. The boat upon deck was full of the sick, covered by an old sail, and the rest were obliged to sit or lie down in any corner where they could find room. The first night was a sickly, suffocating one; and for three more nights and three days (the length of our voyage to Shields), there was little or no amendment of our situation. On board this sloop there were only two beds that were not stowed with goods; and, from my wanting rest so long before I left Edinburgh, I crept into one of them as soon as I could, but found it so low that I could not lie on my side, or easily turn over. So I could get no sleep; and, to mend the matter, I had not been long in this wretched bed till a sucking infant was put in beside me, its mother being dismally sick in the boat upon deck; and the child fell exclusively into my charge. I nursed it as well as I could during the whole voyage; and I think, had I not done so, it must have died. After resting a day or two at South Shields, I set off to Newcastle, where I arrived (in the assize week), I think, on the 12th of August 1776. After my long absence, I found I had a few shillings left. On this occasion, my friends in Newcastle quizzed me not a little for having, as they termed it, begged my way through Scotland.

76

CHAPTER VII

I REMAINED no longer in Newcastle than until I earned as much money as would pay my way to London. I then took my passage on board a collier bound to the great city; and, after beating about in good weather and bad weather for about three weeks, I arrived in London on the 1st October 1776.

The first Cockney I met was the scullerman, who was engaged to land me and my baggage at Carnegie's the hairdresser near Temple Bar. I was amused at his slang and his chatter all the way to London Bridge; and, on approaching it, he asked me if I was 'a-feared'; but, not knowing what I was to be afraid of, I returned the question, at which he looked queer. We passed the gulf* about which he wanted to talk, and I then asked him if he had been 'a-feared'.

It was not long before I found out my old school-fellows, Christopher and Philip Gregson, my old companion, William Gray, then a bookbinder in Chancery Lane, and my friend, Robert Pollard. The first had provided me with a

* [In the sense of whirlpool or eddy.]

lodging, and the last—through the kindness and influence of his master, Isaac Taylor—with plenty of work. Before commencing work, I thought it best to take a ramble through the city and its environs. The first day I went alone, and saw nobody I knew. On the second day, I fell in —by chance—with Sergeant Hymers, in the Strand, who, on seeing me, seemed quite surprised. He held up both his hands—he looked—he laughed—shook me by the hand over and over again, and seemed not to know how to be kind enough. He then took me back with him till he got dressed; and, when this was done, he made a very handsome appearance indeed. The rest of the day he devoted wholly to my service. He first took me to the blackguard places in London. I suppose this was done with a view to corroborate the truth of the stories he had told me before, in Newcastle. After I had seen enough of these places, he took me to others better worth notice; and, having rambled about till I had seen a good deal of the exterior as well as the interior of London—of which it would be superfluous to give an account—I sat down closely to work until I got through the wood-cuts which, through Isaac Taylor's kindness, had been provided for me. I then called upon Thomas Hodgson, printer, George Court, Clerkenwell, who had also provided work for me, to meet my arrival in London, and who had impatiently waited for my assistance. I was subsequently employed by Mr Carnan and Mr Newbery, of St Paul's Church Yard.

Having served my time as a kind of 'jack of all trades', I felt desirous to work amongst the Cockneys, to see if I could find anything amongst them; but in this I was disappointed; for I was never permitted to see any of them at work. They, indeed, seemed desirous of seeing what I was doing, and occasionally peeped in upon me for that purpose. I thought such of them as did so were a most saucy, ignorant, and impudent set. Wherever I went, the ignorant part of the Cockneys called me 'Scotchman'. At this I was not offended; but, when they added other impudent remarks, I could not endure them; and this often led me into quarrels of a kind I wished to avoid, and had not been used to engage in.

It is not worth while noticing these quarrels, but only as they served to help out my dislike to London. They were only trivial compared to other matters. One of the first things that struck me, and that constantly hurt my feelings, was the seeing such a number of fine-looking women engaged in the wretched business of 'street-walking'.* Of these I often enquired as to the cause of their becoming so lost to themselves and to the world. Their usual reply was that they had been basely seduced, and then basely betrayed. This I believed, and was grieved to think that they were thus, perhaps, prevented from becoming the best of mothers to an offspring of lovely and healthy children. I often told them so; and this ended in their tears; and, if they were in poverty, I contributed my mite to relieve them. What a pity it is that this wretchedness is not prevented! Base men treat women as if they were inferior beings, made only to be used like brutes and tyrannized over as slaves. I have always beheld such conduct towards women with abhorrence; for my conceptions of this wretched state of things are of the most soul-harrowing description. It would be extreme weakness to maintain an opinion that all women are good, and that the faults here noticed are always ascribable to the men only. This is not the case; for I am obliged to admit that there are good and bad of each sex. I have often attempted to make an estimate of their comparative numbers, in which I have felt some difficulties. Sometimes my barometer of estimation has

* ['. . . the civil nymph with white-thread stockings who tramps along the Strand and will resign her engaging person to your honour for a pint of wine and a shilling.' Boswell, *London Journal*.]

risen to the height of ten to one in favour of the fair sex; at other times it has fluctuated, and has fallen down some degrees lower in the scale; but, with me, it is now settled, and I cannot go lower than four good women to one good man. I have often wondered how any man could look healthy, beautiful, sensible, and virtuous women in the face without considering them as the link between men and angels. For my part, I have often felt myself so overpowered with reverence in their presence that I have been almost unable to speak, and they must often have noticed my embarrassment. I could mention the names of many, but it might offend their delicacy. When a man can get such a help-mate for life, his happiness must be secured; for such a one is of inestimable value: 'Her price is far above rubies.' I cannot bless them—I would if I could—but may God bless them.

In London one man does one branch of business and another another of the same kind of work, and it is by this division of labour they thus accomplish so much and so well. I however soon tired of working thus, and as I had plenty of work to do on my own account from my former friends to which were added Mr Carnan and Mr Newbery of St Paul's Churchyard. I turned my back upon the masters who took in all kinds of work and stuck to working for myself. Having now been weaned from taking bread and milk, I had learned by degrees to call for a pint of porter, and often spent my evenings at the 'George', in Brook Street,* kept by a person of the name of Darby, whose wife, a very good-looking woman, from Cumberland, claimed a distant relationship to me. At this house, I met with some very respectable and pleasant tradesmen. While I was there one evening, a stranger to me joined us. I think he was a traveller. He had, however, been in Scotland, and had a mighty itch to speak very disrespectfully

* [Close to the Prudential Assurance building in Holborn.]

of that country, and was vociferous in attempting to entertain the company with his account of the filth and dirt he
had met with in it. This I could not bear: their kindness
was fresh in my memory; and I felt resentment rising in
me. I, however, quashed that feeling, and only told him
that I believed I had travelled on foot, perhaps about three
hundred miles through Scotland, and had met with no such
people there, nor such dirtiness as he described. There
might, indeed, be some such in every country for aught I
knew; but I was confident such might be found without
going much beyond the street we were in, and who, in
addition to their filthiness, were also the most wretched
and abandoned of the human race. Some of them, indeed,
appeared to me to be scarcely human. I concluded by observing that I was afraid he had been keeping very bad
company in Scotland. A laugh by this was raised against
him, and he felt himself quashed by his own folly.

I very frequently visited Westminster Abbey, on some
part of the Sunday; and, on the forenoons of that day, I
mostly went with my friend Pollard to hear the Rev ———
Harrison, at St Andrew's Church, Holborn. I sometimes,
also, went to hear eminent preachers at other places. I was
once invited by my friend William Watson, of the
Treasury, who had married the eldest Miss Beilby, to
go with him to hear the Rev Dr Dodd preach at the Mag-
dalen Chapel. Whether this was at the time he was
arrested for forgery I am not certain, but I know I did not
see him. I also went with Mr Watson to hear the Rev ———
Maxwell, another eminent divine; but, indeed, I believe I
did not miss hearing any of the popular preachers in
London.

For many years after I left London, I went to hear the
preachers of various persuasions, and attempted to find out
the general character of their several congregations. Having been brought up under the creeds and doctrines of the

Church of England, I may, perhaps, have some partialities about me respecting that church, but I have ever considered that its clergy are the most learned of any, and that, excepting some of the higher orders of them, they, as well as their hearers, are the most tolerant. I have always felt grieved that a great number of them should consist of very learned and good men with curacies or poor livings that do not afford them a much better income than the wages of common mechanics; and that however great their abilities may be, it is only by patronage that they can be advanced, while enormous stipends are lavished upon others, very often for the most useless, or, perhaps, the most corrupt purposes. I think it would be much better if the incomes of the clergy could be equalized; for, so long as matters are managed otherwise, so long will it be considered as a system of revenue of which religion is only the pretext.

The Roman Catholic mode of faith is the oldest; and they seem the most of any sect attached to it and its old customs and its old creeds, which they seem obstinately to value and persist in, and this most likely will continue so long as they give up their own reason and implicitly obey that dictated to them by their priests. They are the strictest of all disciplinarians in their worship, and are also generally good members of society. The next and most numerous sect are the Methodists, and I fear if they had the upper hand they would soon show a persecuting spirit, but which I hope will never more be suffered to rear its head. This sect took their rise under the able auspices of John Wesley, and at that time he did a great deal of good. In this neighbourhood it was soon made to appear, for he greatly civilized a numerous host of semi-barbarian, the pitmen and others employed in the pit works. These seemed like tribes of Cherokees and Mohawks, but they were more wicked. What I have ever been able to discover of the general character of this sect is that a great number of them are ignorant, bigotted fanatics. Before I left off going to hear them it appeared clear to me that their discourses from the pulpit were mostly unintelligible and the more so this appeared to be, the more numerously were the congregations crowded together to hear such preachers and their jargon. There is another sect growing into great importance as a religious society, and that is the Quakers—the 'Friends' as they properly denominate themselves. They have many excellent rules laid down by which to regulate their conduct in life, and with all their peculiarities, their simplicity of manners commands the respect of the thinking part of mankind. They have, it is true, been characterized as 'English Jews' by some, and others have said of them that they are not now a religious sect like the Methodists—'they are an aristocratic civil community', a trading company, and a set of respectable, industrious, economical, money-getting disciplinarians, who profess no more practical religion than the members of the Church of England. This may no doubt be the opinion of some, but I could never form such a one of, at least, the great majority of them, for they appear to me to deserve a better character. I wish, indeed, to see them leave off a part of their Puritanical appearance, and some other stiffnesses in their deportment. Were all men Quakers, I think the world would have a very sombre appearance, but this is balanced by their keeping their word, by their detestation of war, and by their constant endeavours to live in peace with all men. I have often wondered at their rejecting music. Music is an emanation from heaven; it is perfectly natural to man, to drive away gloom, and to solace and to cheer him. The beautiful choristers of the woods and the fields lead the way and set us the example.

The Unitarians are generally a well informed and respectable description of men. They think for themselves, and are not bewildered with dogmas and creeds. But to swell these opinions of mine with a further account of the peculiarities of each sect, or to attempt to go through the numerous descriptions of religionists would be an endless and a dreary task. They ought each of them to be made welcome to follow their own opinions; and I can only observe that if they are founded in truth, there can be no fear of their being injured by unreserved discussion. Whatever the creed may be, there can be no objecion to the religion of a virtuous man; and it is to be hoped that this opinion will universally prevail and that the distinctions and bickerings amongst different denominations of Christians will cease, and the causes of them be thought of no more importance than whether a man uses his quid of tobacco in the right cheek or in the left.

After this long digression, I must now turn my attention again to London. My friend Mr Watson was very desirous to get me work with Mr Pingo,* in the Mint; and, from his being so well-known and respected by the gentlemen in most of the government offices, he thought this might be easily accomplished. My mind was, however, bent quite another way, and no more was done for me in that business. The constant attention and kindness of my London friends, whose company I enjoyed, was unabated. They walked with me everywhere, and the house of William Gray was a home to me. I met other Newcastle friends, every Monday night, at the 'Hole-in-the-Wall',† Fleet Street, where I went to see the Newcastle newspapers. Some of these occasionally wanted assistance and got my last sixpence. At this time I earned a deal of money; and, from my habits of temperance, I spent little for my own living and thus discovered what a small sum was sufficient to make me independent, and I never lost sight of the

* [Either Thomas or Lewis Pingo, engravers at the Royal Mint.]
† [Resort of Novocastrians in London.]

inestimable value of being so. I, however, never had a surplus of cash long in my possession; for one or another had occasion for it, and I could not bear to see distress without relieving it.

Nothwithstanding my being so situated amongst my friends, and being so much gratified in seeing such a variety of excellent performances in every art and science—painting, statuary, engraving, carving, etc.—yet I did not like London. It appeared to me to be a world of itself, where everything in the extreme might at once be seen: extreme riches, extreme poverty, extreme grandeur, and extreme wretchedness—all of which were such as I had not contemplated before. Perhaps I might, indeed, take too full a view of London on its gloomy side. I could not help it. I tired of it, and determined to return home. The country of my old friends—the manners of the people of that day—the scenery of Tyneside—seemed altogether to form a paradise for me, and I longed to see it again. While I was thus turning these matters over in my mind, my warm friend and patron, Isaac Taylor, waited upon me: and on my telling him I was going to Newcastle, he enquired how long it would be before I returned. 'Never', was my reply; at which he seemed both surprised and displeased. He then warmly remonstrated with me upon this impropriety of my conduct, told me of the prospects before me, and, amongst many other matters, that of his having engaged me to draw in the Duke of Richmond's Gallery;* and he strenuously urged me to change my mind. I told him no temptation of gain, of honour, or of anything else, however great, could ever have any weight with me; and that I would even enlist for a soldier, or go and herd sheep at five shillings per week, as long as I lived, rather than be tied to

* [Charles Lennox, third Duke (1735–1806), had in 1758 opened a gallery in the garden of his house in Whitehall as a free school of painting and sculpture.]

live in London. I told him how sensible I was of his uncommon kindness to me, and thanked him for it. My kind friend left me in the pet, and I never saw him more. He afterwards, when an old man, visited Newcastle, but left it again without my knowing it till after he was gone. At this I felt much grieved and disappointed. I do not remember how long he lived after this; but a memoir of him was published in the 'Analytical Magazine' at the time, together with a letter I had written to him sometime before his death, which he never answered. He was, in his day, accounted the best engraver of embellishments for books, most of which he designed himself. The frontispiece to the first edition of 'Cunningham's Poems' was one of his early productions; and at that time my friend Pollard and myself thought it was the best thing that ever was done.

The same kind persuasions were urged upon me by Mr Hodgson, to remain in London, as had been used by Mr Taylor, which ended in a similar way. The former, however, went further, and told me that, if I were determined upon leaving London, and would continue to work for him in Newcastle, he would furnish me with plenty of it; and that he would begin by giving me as much as would keep me employed for two years. This was particularly pleasing to me, because I could not bear the thoughts of beginning business in Newcastle in opposition to my old master, for whom I had the greatest respect—this to me appeared like 'bring up chickens to pick out your eyes'.

Having spent the evening till a late hour with my friends at the 'George', in Brook Street, and in the morning taken leave of my landlord and landlady, Mr and Mrs Kendal, and their family, in Wharton's Court,* Holborn, I then posted off to the Pool, and got on board a collier; and, after a very short passage, arrived in sight of St Nicholas's Church steeple, about the 22nd June 1777.

* [In a survey map of 1755 it appears as 'Warton Court'.]

CHAPTER VIII

THE first thing after my arrival in Newcastle was to see
my old master, and the next to engage my old lodgings at
Ned Hatfield's, and to fit up a work bench there. I then set
to work upon my wood-cuts. This, however, was interrupted by other jobs; and the first of the kind was that of
engraving a copper plate of the 'Theban Harp', for the Rev
James Murray, for some of his publications. Some of the
silversmiths also began to press their jobs upon me. I had
not, however, been long at work for myself till proposals
were made to me to join in partnership with my late master; and this was brought about by a mutual friend (?),
John Robertson, the silversmith. This proposal—which
was to set me down at once in a well-established business
—I did not relish so warmly as our mutual friend expected.
I had formed a plan of working alone, without apprentices, or being interrupted by anyone; and I am not certain,
at this day, whether I would not have been happier in
doing so than in the way I was led to pursue. I had often,
in my lonely walks, debated this business over in my mind;
but, whether it would have been for the better or the
worse, I can now only conjecture. I tried the one plan, and
not the other: perhaps each might have had advantages and

disadvantages. I should not have experienced the envy and ingratitude of some of my pupils, neither should I, on the contrary, have felt the pride and the pleasure I derived from so many of them having received medals or premiums from the Society for the Encouragement of Arts, and taken the lead, as engravers on wood, in the Metropolis.

Notwithstanding this pride and this pleasure, I am inclined to think I should have had—balancing the good against the bad—more pleasure in working alone for myself than with such help as apprentices afforded, for with some of them I had a deal of turmoil and trouble, and others who shewed capacity and genius, and perhaps served out their time without the interchange of a cross word between us, yet these, from coming under the guidance of people of an envious and malignant disposition, perhaps in unison with their own, were, after every pains and every kindness had been shown to them, when done, ready to strangle me. I have much reason to remember on an occasion of my partner and myself being obliged to take one of the most impudent, malignant, and worst apprentices we ever had before the magistrates, one of them (John Erasmus Blackett, Esq) calling me aside, to enquire if I knew his associates. I told him I did, and he sent for some of them, and in the meantime told me he never knew of any *bad* apprentices being brought before them who had not been spoiled by the wicked advice of some worthless person or other. It is painful to me to dwell upon a subject of this kind, which indeed I might spin out to a great length, with much additional matter, but it may be sufficient to observe, that I have taken a boy and behaved to him uniformly with the kindness of a father or a brother, and have watched with every pains in my power to instruct him, been liberal to him in pecuniary matters, employed the best physician to attend him when he was unwell, let him want for nothing, paid him his wages besides, whether at work or not at work, and in this my partner contributed his share, and along with myself, used every endeavour in our power to advance him in the world, and when all this was done, he showed not a particle of gratitude, but observed that any 'cartman would take care of his Horse', and then put himself under the guidance and directions of a company or confederacy of ill-disposed, envious, and malignant persons, who after having laboured to poison the ears of the public, and of the jury, to bring us to trial for the pay for work done without the leave of his masters while he was our apprentice! and the business was so managed that a verdict was given against us. I did not fail to attack the jury individually, and to send the confederates a message that there was not a man among them who was not a coward and a scoundrel.*

During my absence in London, Mr Beilby had taken an apprentice with a premium; and, to make us equal, I took my brother John as mine. With him I was extremely happy. We lodged together. He rose early in the morning, lighted our fire, blacked our shoes, dusted the room, and made everything clean for breakfast, as well as any servant girl could have done, and he sewed and mended his own clothes, and, to crown all, he was constantly cheerful, lively, and very active, and my friends were his friends. Mr Beilby was as well pleased with him as I could possibly be; for, besides his affable temper, he took every kind of work in hand so pleasantly, and so very soon learned to execute it well, that he could not miss giving satisfaction. This he continued to do as long as he was with us; but other parts of his conduct, when he arrived at manhood, was not so well, and gave me great uneasiness; for he got acquainted with companions whom I thought badly of, and my remonstrances respecting them proved in vain. He would not, as he called it, be dictated to by me; but this I

* [Introduction, p. xxviii.]

persisted in till it made us often quarrel, which was distressing to me, for my regard for him was too deeply rooted ever to think of suffering him to tread in the paths which led to ruin, without endeavouring to prevent it. To the latest day of his life, he repented of having turned a deaf ear to my advice; and as bitterly and sincerely did he acknowledge the slightest obligations he owed me. He *rued*; and that is as painful a word as any in the English language.

As soon as I thought my brother might be able to work his way in the world—he having been, I think, about five years with me—I gave him his liberty, and he set off to London, where, from his reformed conduct and from every information I could learn, he was much liked and respected. He was as industrious in London as he had been with us, and had plenty of work to do. He was almost entirely employed by the publishers and booksellers in designing and cutting an endless variety of blocks for them. He was extremely quick at his work, and did it at a very low rate. His too close confinement, however, impaired his health. He revisited Cherryburn, where he did not remain long till he thought himself quite recovered, and he then returned to London, where he continued a few years longer, and where the same kind of confinement affected his health as before. A similar visit to his native air was found necessary; his health was again restored to him; and again he returned to London. He, however, found that he could not pursue the same kind of close confinement, on which account he engaged to teach drawing at the Hornsey Academy, then kept by Mr Nathaniel Norton, which obliged him to keep a pony to ride backwards and forwards; thus dividing his time between his work-office in London and the school for some years, when his health began again to decline, and he finally left London early in the summer of 1795, and returned once more to the banks of the Tyne. Here he intended to follow the wood engraving for his London friends, and particularly for Wm. Bulmer, for whom he was engaged to execute a number of blocks for the 'Fabliaux' or 'Tales of Le Grand', and for 'Somerville's Chace'. Many of the former he had, I believe, finished in London, and had sketched others on the blocks, which he finished at Cherryburn. He had also sketched the designs on the blocks for the 'Chace'; and to these I put the finishing hand, after his decease, which happened on the 5th of December 1795, aged 35 years. The last thing I could do for him was putting up a stone to his memory at the west end of Ovingham Church, where I hope, when my 'glass is run out', to be laid down beside him.

While my brother was my apprentice, he frequently accompanied me on my weekly visits to Cherryburn. He was then a clever, springy youth, and our bounding along together was often compared to the scamperings of a pair of wild colts. These journeys commenced while I was an apprentice. I then mostly went and returned on the same day; but, when I became my own master, for many years —'in summer's heat and winter's freezing cold'—I did not miss a single week. When I was an apprentice, I had a few holydays at Easter and Whitsuntide allowed me, according to promise; and these were wholly employed in angling; but, after the time came when I might do as I pleased, I mostly stopped, when the weather suited, in spring and summer, and spent the Mondays in various streams, at this my favourite—and, indeed, only diversion. In this I was accompanied by my cheerful associate, 'Jack Roe', with his flies and his tackle; and, when we had got a sufficient number, I returned to Newcastle with my creel well filled with fish, which I divided amongst my friends. With an account of these hungry, stream-wading ramblings, and the days spent in angling, and with a description of the beautiful scenery of water-sides, and the renovating charms which these altogether inspired, a volume might be filled, in imitation of the patriarch of anglers, Izaak Walton: as might also one of a descriptive or sentimental journal of these my weekly visits to my parents. These visits continued regularly from 1777 till 1785, in which year my mother, my eldest sister, and my father, all died.

It will readily be believed that, if I had not felt uncommon pleasure in these journeys, I would not have persisted in them; nor in facing the snow storms, the floods, and the dark nights of so many winters. This, to some, appeared like insanity, but my stimulant, as well as my reward, was in seeing my father and mother in their happy home. I always reflected that this would have an end, and that the time would come when I should have no feelings of warm regard called up on their account. Besides these gratifications, I felt others in observing the weekly changes of the long-lengthened and varied year, which, by being so measured out, appeared like living double one's time. The 'Seasons', by the inimitable Thomson, had charmed me greatly; but, viewing nature thus experimentally, pleased me much more. To be placed in the midst of a wood in the night, in whirlwinds of snow, while the tempest howled above my head, was sublimity itself, and drew forth aspirations to Omnipotence such as had not warmed my imagination so highly before; but, indeed, without being supported by ecstasies of this kind, the spirits, beset as they were, would have flagged, and I should have sunk down.

As soon as the days began to lengthen, and the sprouting herbage had covered the ground, I often stopped with delight by the sides of woods, to admire the dangling woodbine and roses, and the grasses powdered or spangled with pearly drops of dew; and also, week after week, the continued succession of plants and wild flowers. The prim-

rose, the wild hyacinth, the harebell, the daisy, the cow-
slip, etc.—these, altogether, I thought no painter ever
could imitate. I had not, at that time, ever heard the name
of the great and good Linnaeus, and knew plants only by
their common English names. While admiring these beau-
tifully-enamelled spots on my way, I was also charmed
with the equally beautiful little songsters, which were constantly pouring out their various notes to proclaim the
spring. While this exhilarating season glided on by im-
perceptible degrees, unfolding its blossoms till they faded
into summer, and as the days lengthened, my hours of
rising became more and more early. I have often thought,
that not one-half of mankind knew anything of the beauty,
the serenity, and the stillness of the summer mornings in
the country, nor have ever witnessed the rising sun's
shining forth upon the new day.

I had often listened with great pleasure and attention to
my father's description of the morning, with his remarks
upon the various wild quadrupeds and the strange birds
he had seen or heard in these still hours throughout the
year; for he left his bed very early in summer, and seldom
later than four or five o'clock in the winter. The autumn
I viewed as the most interesting season, and, in its appearance, the most beautiful. It is then that the yellow harvest
of the fields, and the produce of the orchards, are gathered
in, as the reward of the labours of the year; while the picturesque beauties and varying foliage of the fading woods,
with their falling leaves, and the assembling in flocks of
the small birds, put me in mind of the gloomy months
with which the year is closed.

This is the short account of many years of uninterrupted
health, buoyant spirits, and of great happiness to me. I had
begun betimes, and by degrees, to habituate myself to temperance and exercise, which hardened the constitution to
such a pitch that neither wet nor cold had any bad effect

upon me. On setting out upon my weekly pedestrian 'flights' up the Tyne, I never looked out to see whether it was a good day or a bad one; the worst that ever fell from the skies never deterred me from undertaking my journey. On setting out, I always waded through the first pool I met with, and had sometimes the river to wade at the far end. I never changed my clothes, however they might be soaked with wet, or stiffened by the frost, on my returning home at night, till I went to bed. I had inured myself to this hardship, by always sleeping with my windows open, by which a thorough air, as well as the snow, blew through my room. In this way, I lay down, stripped into 'bare buff' except being rolled in a blanket, upon a mattress as hard as I could make it. Notwithstanding this mode of treating myself, I never had any ailment, even in the shape of a cold, while I continued to live in this way; nor did I experience any difference until, when I married, I was obliged to alter my plans, and to live and behave like other folks. If persons brought up and habituated to the tender indulgences common in the world, and not trained by degrees to bear the mode of life I have been describing were to try it, unprepared, the experiment would be at their peril. My travelling expenses for the day were commonly only a penny or twopence for crossing the water. On the hottest day, I was never made violently to perspire, but only felt a dampness on my brow. I carried no useless weight of fat about me, and the muscular parts were as hard as it was possible to be on any human being. On being asked by a gentleman—an acquaintance whom I met at Ovingham—what I got to drink on such hot days, on my road, my reply was—'Nothing'. He had not been used to such doings himself; and was surprised, and could hardly believe me. He earnestly persuaded me to try the experiment of the amazing good a glass of brandy and water would do me in hot weather. This I took no notice of for some time: at length, however, on a thundery, hot day, on being scorched with heat, and in danger of being struck with lightning, which darted from a sky almost as black as ink, I stepped into a public-house in Crawcrook, and, for the first time in my life, called for a glass of brandy and water. I was then about 28 years old—and surely I thought this brandy and water was the most delicious beverage in the world. This would not be worth noticing, but only on account of its being a beginning to me, and which I did not, when occasion pressed me, leave off for some years afterwards. I often called in, almost every Sunday morning, for my glass, while my route lay on that side of the river, and until being quizzed for visiting 'Maggy Hay's bonny lasses'. I then left off, and walked up the north side of the Tyne, and crossed at Wylam, Ovingham, or Eltringham boat; and now only sometimes at Scotswood, when I had occasion to visit my friends at Hedley, but indeed I varied my roundabout ways in these journeys, pursuing the one I had haunted myself to, for perhaps a quarter of a year to an end, before I left it off, and thus became known to most of the villages on both banks of the Tyne, and as nothing can pass unnoticed in villages, so they noticed me, and set it down for granted that I was sweethearting some pretty female on my way. This life of rapturous enjoyment has its acids, and at length comes to an end; and so did my walks, and my contemplations, or reflections, which passed through the mind while engaged in them. These, at the time, were mostly communicated to a moralizing, and sensibly religious friend, Joseph Hubbuck, who waited my return on the Sunday evenings, when, over our supper of a pint of ale and a cake, for each, he, in return, detailed to me the import of the sermons he had heard through the day.

CHAPTER IX

In Christmas week, 1784, while I was on some errand to Ovingham, amusing myself with sliding on the ice, as smooth almost as a looking-glass, between Eltringham and that place—I know not what came over my mind, but something ominous haunted it, of a gloomy change impending over the family. At this I was surprised, for I had never before felt any such sensation, and presently scouted it as some whim of the imagination. The day was to be one of cheerfulness; for Mr and Mrs Storey—distant relations of my father, and for whom my parents had the greatest regard—had been, with other friends, invited to dine with us at Cherryburn. At dinner all was kindness and cheerfulness, and my father was, as usual, full of his jokes, and telling some of his facetious stories and anecdotes. For two, or perhaps three Sundays after this, I was prevented from getting over the water, by the ice and other floods, and returned from Ovingham without seeing or hearing how all were at home. The Sunday after, upon my making my usual call at John Gilchrist's, the gardener in Ovingham—where, when at school, we always left our dinner poke, and dined—he informed me, with looks of grief, that my mother was very unwell. I posted off, in haste, along with him, and across the river to see her. Upon my asking her, earnestly, how she was, she took me apart, and told me it was nearly all over with her; and she described to me how she had got her death. She had been called up, on a severe frosty night, to see a young woman in the hamlet below, who was taken ill; and, thinking the bog she had to pass through might be frozen hard enough to bear her, she 'slumped' deep into it, and, before she had waded through it, she got very wet and a 'perishment' of cold; and, in that state, she went to give her advice as to what was best to be done with her patient. I employed my friend, Dr Bailes, to visit her; and I ran up from Newcastle two or three times a week with his medicines for her; but all would not do; she died on the 20th February 1785, aged 58 years. She was possessed of great innate powers of mind, which had been cultivated by a good education, as well as by her own endeavours. For these, and for her benevolent, humane disposition, and good sense, she was greatly respected, and, indeed, revered by the whole neighbourhood. My eldest sister, Hannah Chambers, who was down from London on a visit to her home, at the time of my mother's illness and death, by her over-exertion and anxiety, brought on a miscarriage and became very ill; and, for the convenience of medical aid, and better nursing, I brought her to my hitherto little happy cot, at the Forth, where she died on the 24th June 1785, aged 30 years. These were gloomy days to me! Some short time before my sister died, upon her requesting me, and my promising her, that I would see her buried at Ovingham, she proposed to sing me a song. I thought this very strange, and felt both sorrow and surprise at it; but she smiled at me, and began her song of 'All Things have but a Time'. I had heard the old song before, and thought pretty well of it; but hers was a later and a very much better version of it.

During this time I observed a great change in the looks and deportment of my father. He had, what is called, 'never held up his head' since the death of my mother; and, upon my anxiously pressing him to tell me what ailed him, he said he had felt as if he were shot through from the breast to the shoulders with a great pain that hindered him from breathing freely. Upon my mentioning medical assistance, he rejected it, and told me, if I sent him any drugs, I might depend upon it he would throw them all behind the fire. He wandered about all summer alone, with a kind of serious look, and took no pleasure in anything, till near the 15th November, which, I understand, was his birthday, and on which he completed his 70th year, and on that day he died. He was buried beside my mother and sister at Ovingham. After this, I left off my walks to Cherryburn; the main attractions to it were gone; and it became a place the thoughts of which now raked up sorrowful reflections in my mind. Some particulars respecting my father, and illustrative of his character, may, perhaps, be thought not uninteresting. I shall give a few of such as I recollect them. In his person, he was a stout, square-made, strong, and active man, and through life was a pattern of health. I was told by some of my aunts, who were older than he, that he was never ill from a disease in his life; and I have heard him say 'he wondered how folks felt when they were bad'. He was of a cheerful temper, and he possessed an uncommon vein of humour and a fund of anecdote. He was much noticed by the gentlemen and others of the neighbourhood for these qualities, as well as for his integrity. He had, however, some traits that might be deemed singular, and not in order. He never would prosecute anyone for theft; he hated going to law, but he took it at his own hand, and now and then gave thieves a severe beating, and sometimes otherwise punished them in a singular and whimsical way. I have known him, on a winter night, rise suddenly up from his seat, and, with a stick in his hand, set off to the colliery, in order to catch the depredators whom he might detect stealing his coals. I remember one instance of his thus catching a young fellow, a farmer with his loaded cart, and of his giving him a severe beating, or, what was called, a 'hideing', and of his making him leave his booty and go home empty. The thieves themselves were sure to keep the business secret, and he himself never spoke of it beyond his own fireside. In these robberies, which he saw with his own eyes, he conceived he did not need the help of either witnesses, judge, or jury, nor the occasion to employ any attorney to empty his pockets. I have sometimes heard him make remarks upon people whom he knew to be hypocrites, and on their loud praying and holding up their hands at church. After having noticed that one of these, one Sunday, had acted thus, and remained to take the Sacrament, some person called, in the afternoon, with the news that this very man had, on his way home, caught the galloway of poor Tommy Cook the shoemaker, which had entered through a gap in the hedge into his field, and had driven it before him into the pinfold. This was sufficient; this was the spark which kindled up and increased to a blaze, which my father could not muster temper enough to keep down. Next morning, he set off to the smith's shop, and sent for this choleric, purse-proud man, to whom, in rude terms, he opened out upon his hypocrisy, and at length obliged him to release the galloway from its hungry imprisonment. He recommended him to make his peace with the poor but honest and respected man, and to go no more to church, nor to take the Sacrament, till a change had taken place in his mind. He also told him that he ought that very night, before he slept, to sit down on his bare knees, and implore forgiveness of the God of truth, justice and mercy for his past crimes.

The last transaction I shall mention, on this subject—and which bore a more serious complexion than the foregoing—happened when I was an apprentice. A pitman, George Parkin, who had long wrought in the colliery, was highly valued by my father for his industry, sobriety, and honesty. He would not do anything unfairly himself in working the coal in the boards, nor suffer others to do so. For this conduct he became deservedly a great favourite—so much so that one of the old lodges had been comfortably fitted up for him and his family to live in rent free; and a garth, besides, was taken off the common for his use. For these he often expressed himself so highly pleased that he used to say, he was happier than a prince. My father, for many years—ever indeed, since the gin once ran amain, and, in his attempting to stop it, he got his skull fractured—had made it a point, if possible, to let the men down to their work himself; so that he might see with his own eyes that all was safe. All passed on pleasantly in this way for a long while, till one morning, when thus employed letting the men down, George, who was always the first at his work, having fixed himself on the chain, with his son on his arm, to be both let down together, had given the signal, 'Wise-away', and at the same time holding up his 'low-rope', he observed the pit rope which was to bear their weight had been cut near the chain. On this he shouted 'Stop' and started back upon the 'seddle boards', just in time to prevent himself and the boy from being precipitated to the bottom of the pit. The poor man was almost over-powered with the shock, when my father, keeping the 'dreg' upon the 'start', caught hold of him and the boy, and conducted both into the lodge. On examining the rope, my father found it had been cut through to the last strand. He then stopped the working of the pit for that day. Poor Geordy, in great distress of mind, set off to Newcastle to inform me of what had happened. I was grieved to hear his tale; and this was heightened by his declaring that all his pleasures were at an end; for he never could go back to his work, nor to his happy home again.*

* ['Indeed, before 1815, it was not the custom to hold inquests on deaths in the mines of Northumberland and Durham.' G. M. Trevelyan, *History of England*.]

For some time, my father seemed lost in pondering over this mysterious affair. He, however, at length began to be fixed in his suspicions, and, as was usual on such occasions, his indignation, step by step, rose to the greatest height. In this state of mind, he set off unusually soon in the morning, to let the men down to their work; knowing that the object of his suspicions—a wicked, ignorant, young fellow—would be the first, and alone. He began by accusing him of the horrid deed, and instantly to beat and overpower him; threatening him that he would drag him to the pit, and throw him down the shaft, if he did not confess. The threat succeeded: he was afraid of his life, and confessed. My father instantly dismissed him from his employment. When the rest of the men came to their work, they saw, by the blood, and the retaliating blows on my father's face, that something unusual had occurred. He then told them the particulars, at which they greatly rejoiced. In this state of things, the accusing culprit, while he bore the marks of violence upon him, set crippling off to lodge his complaint to the justices, and my father was summoned to appear before them. When met together, the justices (Captains Smith and Bainbridge, of the Riding) heard the charge of assault, which, from the first appearance of the complainant before them, they had no reason to doubt. They both expressed their surprise to find such a charge against my father, with whom they had been in habits of neighbourly intimacy, and who was the last man on earth they could suspect as capable of committing such an outrage. After laying down the law in such cases, they wished to hear what he had to say for himself. He readily acknowledged what he had done, and his reasons for doing so. They seemed much shocked at the horrid narrative; and, after conferring together in private a short time, the business was resumed. 'Pray,' said one of them to the culprit, 'were not you the man who robbed Bywell Lock, and'

—looking him sternly in the face—'was not this master of yours the very friend by whose unceasing endeavours and influence you were saved from transportation? Begone! leave the country, and never let us see you more.' The man left the country for many years, and, on his return, I was both pleased and surprised to find he was much reformed. In addition to this long account, I must add, that my father could not be troubled to harbour ill-will in his mind, and that, if he were passionate, he was equally compassionate.

CHAPTER X

FOR many years, including a part of those of my apprenticeship, my master and self were fully employed upon such work as I have named before, from silversmiths, watchmakers, and hardware-men; but a new customer (Isaac Hymen, a Jew) came in the way with his seal-cutting orders, which amounted to more, in that way, than all the rest put together. This man, besides his box of watches, trinkets, etc., had gathered together a large collection of impressions of well-cut seals; and, being a man of good address, and a good singer, had introduced himself into coffee-rooms frequented by gentlemen and respectable tradesmen, where he exhibited his impressions as the work of his own hands; and, by this management—for he knew nothing whatever of engraving—he got orders. Somehow or other, it was propagated throughout the town that his seals surpassed by far anything we ever did, or could do; and, although we had done the whole of his orders, this was believed, and there seemed to be only one opinion as to his very superior excellence. I remember once rising early in the morning, and working till late at night, and, on that day, cutting five steel seals with cyphers and initials, for which our common wholesale charge was 3s. 6d., and to our private customers, 5s. For these he charged

12s. 6d. each to his friends. He observed to me, on my remarking to him on his extravagant charges, 'that it was foolish in us to do as we did'; and, for himself, he said, 'you know, I must live'. My wages for the short time I worked for my master, after I was out of my apprenticeship, was a guinea per week, but Isaac offered me two guineas if I would travel with him. The travelling part I should have liked well enough, but not to travel with a Jew. He went on in this way, with his orders, till we had no other customer in that department; and my master then, as well as when I became his partner, often expressed himself highly chagrined that some of his old private friends went past him, and even joined others in lessening our work. Our friend Isaac continued long uninterruptedly thus to carry all before him, till some of our old customers became irritated at him, and particularly John Harrison, the watchmaker, who took great pains to open out and expose the business. Isaac then left Newcastle, and report said he was found dead on the road between Sunderland and Durham. I have often seen, in London—and perhaps the same may be observed in every large town—'The pale artist ply his sickly trade', to keep in affluence such managing, money-making, pretended artists as Isaac Hymen; and this must continue to be the case so long as gentlemen will not go themselves to the fountain head, and be at the pains to encourage merit.

Our main supporters in the silver engraving were John Langlands and his partner John Robertson. Before they entered into partnership, Mr Robertson was well known and much respected in almost every principal town in Britain, and (I believe) in Ireland, as a travelling silversmith and jeweller, and by his superior knowledge of business he greatly augmented that of their joint concern. Mr Langlands was of a cheerful, hospitable, and charitable disposition, full of stories and anecdotes, and that kind of man who greatly esteemed men of ability, integrity, and industry. These he never forgot when age or infirmities brought them down. He then shook hands with them as he had done before, but his own mostly concealed his token of respect—a half-guinea. Mr Robertson, was also, in many respects, of a similar disposition to his partner. I spent many a cheerful evening in Mr Langlands' house, in company with others who also partook of his hospitable board. The most remarkable of these was Matthew Prior, who had the character of being one of the best mechanics in the kingdom. He was assay master, a musical instrument maker, and a turner, in which last he particularly excelled. The many remarkable pieces of dexterous workmanship he had done in that way drew upon him the notice of many gentlemen in the two northern counties, with whom also, as an angler, a sportsman, and a jovial companion, he was a welcome guest. It happened, on some pretence or other, that an attempt was made to take away the assay business from Newcastle, which occasioned Prior to be sent for, to be examined by (I believe) a committee of the House of Commons, as to his ability in conducting that business. The ease, the clearness, as well as the straightforward way in which he answered all questions excited some surprise, as well as approbation. When questioned as to the accuracy of his scale-beam, he said a hair clipped from the back of his hand would turn his scales either way. For a wager, he turned two billiard balls of such equal weights that the difference was as nothing. He was of a most independent cast of character, and open and frank in his conversation. It had been reported that Prior had said of a proud, high-minded gentleman that 'he durst do what neither the gentleman nor any of his family dared do'. Prior had never said any such thing; but this gentleman took him to task about it, and, with great indignation, accused him of saying so. At this, Prior, in his turn, felt offended, and told him, though he had never said so, he would now say so to his face. This produced a wager between them; and Matthew told him he would double the bet if he pleased. 'Now,' said the gentleman, in high ill-humour, 'what is it you dare do?' 'Do!' said Prior, 'I dare spend the last sixpence I have in the world!'

During a great part of the time I have been noticing, the American War was going on. The 'press' broke out just after I landed in London, and, to escape the gang, one of our crew came and took refuge with me. This poor fellow, a decent man, had in his youth been on board a ship of war; and, as far as concerned himself, he said he did not mind going again; but the thoughts of being dragged from his family threw him into very great distress. Political writings and debatings sometimes ran very high between those who were advocates for a system of corruption, and profited by the taxes, and those who were advocates for the liberties of mankind; but it always appeared to me that a very great majority of the people were decidedly against the war. These writings and debatings, which the war occasioned, certainly served greatly to alter the notions and the opinions of the people respecting the purity of the British government, and its representative system; and this attempt at doing it away altogether in America seemed a prelude to the same system of misrule, when, by slower degrees, a future opportunity offered for doing it away at home. In these political debatings, the question was often asked, 'Whether the government was made for the people, or the people for the government?' Great numbers, who hoped for the best, still clung to the government under which they had been brought up, and had been taught to revere as excellency itself. While others were contending whether a kingly government or a republic was best, it was generally admitted that a deal might be said *pro* and *con*; for many examples might be adduced of mal-

106

administration under both forms. Some of these disputants
would repeat what Pope had said—

> 'For modes of faith let graceless zealots fight,
> His can't be wrong whose life is in the right;
> For forms of government, it is confest
> That which is best administered is best.'

In England the people may boast that their forefathers
had a king, in Alfred the Great, the wisest, the bravest, and
the best the world ever knew; by whose excellent conduct
was laid the foundation of the liberties of his country, and
from the influence of which there can be no doubt that the
English language will be spoken over the whole Globe.
Were kings to endeavour to follow his example, and ever
to keep in mind that they and their ministers ought to
consider themselves as a royal society for the promotion
of arts and sciences, and of everything that can enlighten
the minds and ameliorate the condition of mankind, they
would do right. Kings would then reign in the hearts of
the great overwhelming mass of the people, and no confederacy or conspiracy of nobles or others could ever upset
their rule. But, while they continue to suffer themselves to
be surrounded by flatterers, sycophants, and selfish knaves,
no good need be expected; for they are thus brought up
like petted children, and have not the same chance of becoming wise as other men. Thus situated, they are to be
pitied. One would think that the respectable part of the
old nobility, or other opulent men of great abilities, might
be found with patriotism enough to perform the offices of
the ministry gratis, scorning high salaries and only looking
to honourable distinction. This would of itself put an end
to corruption. Justices of the peace take the very great
trouble of acting their parts gratuitously; churchwardens
and overseers do the same; and why do not the great and
rich men of the land follow the praiseworthy example?

In turning back to take another look at the American

war, one may reckon to a certainty of its having been made the subject of debatings, and of furnishing matter for the thinking part of mankind, over the whole of the civilized world. George the Third and his advisers did not, perhaps, think of this, nor its consequences; neither did they ever contemplate the mighty events they were thus bringing about in rearing and establishing the wisest and greatest republic and nation the world ever saw. When its immense territory is filled with an enlightened population, and its government, like a rock, founded on the liberties and the rights of man, it is beyond human comprehension to foresee the strides the nation will make towards perfection. It is likely they will cast a compassionate eye on the rest of the world, grovelling under arbitrary power, banish it from the face of the earth, and kill despots with a frown. One would fain hope, however, that kings and their advisers will coolly reflect upon the improving intellect of mankind, and take measures to govern in a way more befitting the state of the people over whom they are called upon to rule.

During the long continuance of this war, and the debatings as before noticed, I became acquainted with a number of genteel young men of a literary turn, who kept a library of books, and held their meetings in a room at Sam. Alcock's, at the sign of the Cannon, at the foot of the old Flesh Market, and I used to frequent this house in the evenings to get my pint of ale and a cake, and to hear the news and to have a bit of chat or conversation with some of them when they adjourned from their book society. I did not join their society, but I sometimes dined with them at their annual, cheerful dinner. I was never fond of public dinners or dining parties; and I think I would not have partaken with them had I not been tempted to do so by way of hearing their songs, with which I felt much charmed, but particularly with the Scotch songs, with which one of the members, Walter Cannaway the carver and gilder, used so highly to delight the company on these occasions. He, according to my notions, was the best singer I ever heard. I have always been more charmed with the human voice, when well attuned, than with any instrumental music whatever; and his voice was extremely good. He could in a natural tone go to the highest and the lowest pitch, with his pauses, his shakes or quavers, all in time. Many others, perhaps, might have as good a voice, and as correct an ear for music as he, and would have been equally as charming had they not been spoiled by the fashion they had got into to please the surfeited tastes of coxcombical connoisseurs and a vitiated, aping public. I have ever been much disgusted to hear and see these spoiled performers, quavering and spinning out their unnatural falsetto voices until almost spent. It showed well how long-winded these kind of performers were, but I never could sit to hear any of them; as it appeared to me to be anything but music, or music run mad.

On my first going to business, I had an opportunity of sometimes hearing musical concerts. My master belonged to a musical society held at Moore's in the Close, and when I had any message to take to him, I was commonly invited to remain. The two sons of Charles Avison, the great musical composer, belonged to this society, and Mr Beilby and family were on terms of intimacy with them. I also occasionally heard the band at the theatre, but I cannot say I felt much pleasure in listening to them, and I well remember on one occasion of setting them aside. The late Mr Dibden, who often called upon me, had some performance to exhibit at our theatre, and had quarrelled with the theatrical band on account of their exorbitant demands; and, in this dilemma, he expressed himself much disappointed, and knew not what to do. I told him I thought, if he would leave the matter to me, I could set all right; and I instantly applied to old Wm. Lamshaw, the Duke of Northumberland's piper, to play at the theatre. I being well acquainted with the old man, he readily assented. I then told my friend Dibden what I had done, and satisfied him as to the preference the audience would give to the piper. In this I was not mistaken; for all went well off, and everyone expressed both pleasure and surprise at the change.

Some time before the American war broke out, there had been a lack of musical performers in our streets, and in this interval, I used to engage John Peacock, our inimitable performer, to play on the Northumberland or small pipes; and with his old tunes, his lilts, his pauses, and his variations, I was always excessively pleased. At one time I was afraid that these old tunes, and this ancient instrument might, from neglect of encouragement, get out of use, and I did everything in my power to prevent this, and to revive it, by urging Peacock to teach pupils to become masters of this kind of music; and I flatter myself that my efforts were not lost. I was suspicious that the Northumberland family were beginning to feel indifferent, or to overlook and slight these their ancient minstrels, who had for ages past been much esteemed, and kept in attendance by their forefathers. It was, however, with great pleasure I found that they had appointed William Cant, a pupil of old William Lamshaw, to be piper to the Northumberland Regiment of Militia; and he kept up with great spirit and effect this department of their music while he remained in the regiment. Nor was the regiment behind in the other departments of music; for it was allowed by judges that their fifers and drummers were inferior to none in the kingdom. One man, in particular—John Bowman—it was asserted, was the best performer on the fife that was 'known in the world'. Certain it is that every year for twenty-two years, he challenged the fifers of every regiment stationed in Newcastle, to a trial of skill on that instrument; but none of them could compete with him. He could draw out tones from it the most soft and graceful, as well as the most stunning and loud, such as the ear could not endure in a room, and which were only fit to be heard in the open air.

CHAPTER XI

I HAVE noticed several of my friends and acquaintances whose characters stood high in my estimation. I have now another to introduce, the play-fellow of my youth, Thomas Lawson, as remarkable as any of them. He left Tyneside, his and my home, and came to Newcastle about 1777 or '78, to launch out into the world of exertion and turmoil; and, from his abilities and integrity, he seemed well befitted to make a great figure in it, and, had he been spared, he would, in my opinion, have shone out like another Benjamin Franklin. He was for a short time one of my schoolfellows at Ovingham; but, from his father having been beggared by the failure of a coalowner for whom he had been employed many years, my young friend was obliged to leave school, and to seek out some employment for himself, while his mother brought up a large family with the small profits of a public house, the sign of the White Horse in Ovingham. The house was his father's, but the brewer got it for what was owing to him for ale. This brewer, however, being a generous man, still did not take the house as his own, but permitted the family to keep it, for the support of themselves and some of the younger children. In the interim, he took up his abode in my father's house as a home, his mother having been much respected by my mother, a close intimacy having long subsisted between them. The first employment that my companion got was that of a plough-driver. He next became a farmer's servant, and afterwards a manager of a farm and brewery. In all these departments, he was distinguished for his industry, good sense, good management, and great integrity. It happened, however, that he, being handsome in his person and manly in his deportment, his employer began to suspect that the young lady of the house was showing a marked partiality towards him; and this having occasioned some frowns and hints which his spirit could not brook, he gave up the place. Having seen an advertisement from a gentleman going on his travels, who wanted a young man as a servant and a manager of his affairs, poor Lawson was struck with this as a thing worth looking after, and he immediately set off to Newcastle to make the necessary enquiries. For that purpose he waited upon Mr Slack, bookseller and editor of the *Newcastle Chronicle*. As soon as he entered the shop or office, Mrs Slack eyed him from head to foot; and, after a short pause, she broke silence and began by telling him she thought it a great pity that such a young man, as he appeared to be, should not do better than putting himself to be a gentleman's servant, and asked him if he would not like better to be* some trade or business. This he readily admitted, but at the same time observed, that he had not the means of doing so. Being a very sensible clever woman, she told him she would endeavour to help him to accomplish this, and after some bargain-making it was agreed that he was for a few years to be bound to Mr Slack as a pressman, for which he was to be paid eight shillings per week. At that time and with

* ['Put to' or 'bound to' inadvertently omitted by Bewick?]

this wage, he contrived to maintain himself and to pay out of it for a night-school education, under the Rev John Baillie. His progress was truly astonishing in figures, languages, the use of the globes, etc.; but his memory was so tenacious that he retained whatever he learned, and he could repeat the longest harangue (as far as I was able to judge) verbatim. I once had an opportunity of witnessing this, in his repeating the whole of a charity sermon, preached by the eloquent the Rev Dr Scott, of Simonburn. While he was employed in the drudgery of the printing press, he, at the same time, made himself master of the business of a compositor, and presently became a secondary foreman or manager under Robert Carr, who had long conducted the business in that office. I do not recollect how long he remained in Mr Slack's employment, but shortly after he left him, he married a young woman of respectable parentage, who had long been in love with him. It happened that the printing of a Bible in numbers had been established; but the editor, either from mismanagement, or something amiss, was on the verge of a failure. In this state of affairs, Lawson turned his attention to the business, and applied to his wife's friends for assistance, but they could, at that time, only spare him about thirty pounds; and with this sum in hand, he made a proposal for purchasing the types, and everything belonging to the printing office. It is singular enough that the printer referred to, having left Newcastle, lived and had his printing office in the governor's house at Tynemouth, whither I went with my friend when the bargain was closed between them. He now commenced business on his own account, but how long he had to struggle through difficulties, before he got well established, I have forgotten. It is remarkable that he met with unsolicited aid from many friends; for every one who knew him became interested in his welfare. He lived till he surmounted every obstacle to his prosperity; but, in doing this, his too great application and exertion ruined his health. He pined away and died, in a house close by mine at the Forth, on the 7th March 1783, aged 31 years. I, with many other of his friends, accompanied his remains to Ovingham, where he was buried. This was the first time in my life that I felt poignant grief.

My old schoolfellow and friend, Philip Gregson, of the Custom House, London, being on a visit to his relatives and friends in the north, in 1780, I, being fond of rambling, proposed setting him on his return home, as far as York, if he would walk with me to that city, to which he agreed; and, after spending a day or two with him there, we parted. On my return, I took the road by Boroughbridge to Ripon, where I stayed a short time till I had viewed the country round it, and particularly Studley Park and its beautiful scenery. I then returned to Darlington, and changed my route to the westward, by Barnard Castle, Bowes, over Stainmore to Brough, Appleby, and Penrith; and from thence to my uncle's at Ainstable. On leaving him and his family, I walked home that day to Cherryburn, and so on the next to Newcastle.

I have not interlarded this journey with any of my remarks on the road—on the grandeur of York Minster—the large upright stones called 'The Devil's Arrows', near Boroughbridge—the extensive prospects from Cross Fell, etc.; and therefore my dear Jane must regard the whole of this merely as one of my 'tramps', and a description of these places by others may be referred to.

In another of my perambulations, I prevailed on my acquaintance, Walter Cannaway, to accompany me to Berwick. We set off on an Easter Sunday morning, in 1784, by the seaside, and our first halt was at Chevington, beyond Widdrington. I had not broken my fast, and was quite ready to make a hearty meal upon some dry barley cake and cheese, whilst my thirsty companion, with equal pleasure, enjoyed himself with hearty draughts of ale. We reached Lesbury in the afternoon, and, when my fellow-traveller sat down, he observed, that I might go on if I pleased, but he would not move a foot further that night. Next day, after sauntering about a little in the villages on our road, we reached Elwick, the hospitable mansion of my friend Thomas Younghusband Esq., where we stopped that night. Mr Younghusband happened to have a few of his friends to spend the evening with him. We got on to make merry and to sing songs; and, when it came to Cannaway's turn, the party were so agreeably surprised and pleased at his performance that we did not separate till the morning. My companion and I set off to Berwick, and, after seeing the town, we returned to Elwick by Holy Island. In the performance of this day's journey we had to encounter some difficulties which might have been attended with fatal consequences. We had been cautioned against attempting, after a certain hour, to walk across the extensive flat left bare by the ebb tide. We were beyond the time named, but resolved to proceed, and had to run the greatest part of the way; and it was well we did so; for, before we reached the Island, we found the tide was rapidly advancing between us and the shore, and we had to wade deeply before we reached it. On looking back, over the flat space we had just left, we were surprised to view it as a sea. My companion, being rather corpulent, was in a sad state of perspiration with over exertion, and I think I was not much better, from the anxiety I felt for him, while I was constantly urging him to mend his speed. We now hastened to a public-house, dripping with wet, where my companion took a few glasses of gin, and prevailed on me to take one along with him; and this is the first glass of that liquor I ever recollect taking. Our next business was to get a boat to set us across the arm of the sea, between the island and the nearest shore, towards Elwick. It was then nearly dark;

and, before the boatmen got us rowed across, it was quite so. Where they landed us we knew not, but we had to wade to the dry beach. In shaping our course to Elwick, we lost ourselves in the fields, and it was late before we arrived there. We were in as dirty a state as wet and mire could make us. Mrs Younghusband, however, lost no time in fitting us up with dry clothes, and in making us as comfortable as she could. I remained a day or two at Elwick, and made some visits along with Mr Younghusband in the neighbourhood. My fellow-traveller had somewhat similar visits to pay, in collecting some debts due to him, which, when done, he met me at Alnwick, where Mr Younghusband having to attend a meeting of freeholders, on some election business, at the town hall, I accompanied him thither. Never having before heard any speeches, I was much entertained with those now made. This being about the time that Mr Pitt came into the administration, and being the son of the great Chatham, most people hoped and expected he would follow the bright, the patriotic example that had been set him; but one gentleman appeared to differ in opinion from the majority, and, in what I conceived to be an eloquent speech, foretold that he would turn out, in character, to be quite a different kind of man.

About the year 1790, I became a member of 'Swarley's Club', held in the evenings, at the Black Boy Inn. This was the most rational society or meeting I ever knew. The few rules which bound us together were only verbal. The first was that every member should conduct himself with decorum, and as a gentleman. If anyone transgressed on this point, he was immediately fined, and if he did not pay, he was sent to Coventry, or dismissed. On entering the room, every member paid fourpence, which was to be spent in beer only. Any member might introduce his friend at the same expense. There were no fines for non-attendance and no regular debatings allowed on any subject but such as might occasionally arise out of the passing conversation, and the company separated at ten o'clock. George Carlton was perpetual President, and in that office always conducted himself in a pleasant and gentlemanly manner. William Preston, the printer, was Secretary and Treasurer, and always acquitted himself in the same agreeable way the president had done. Conversations amongst the friends thus associated—consisting of merchants, or respectable tradesmen—were carried on without restraint, and only interrupted for the moment while the president claimed attention to any particular news of the day that might be worth notice. Such a place of meeting proved convenient and pleasant to many a stranger who visited the town, and the expense was as nothing. It may seem strange that, out of a fourpenny club like this, there was commonly an overplus left, to give away at Christmas and Easter to some charitable purpose. I went to this club when I had time to spare in an evening, and seldom missed a week to an end. This happy society was at length broken up, at the time when war on behalf of despotism was raging, and the spy system was set afloat. Some spies, and others of the same stamp, contrived to get themselves introduced, and to broach political questions, for the purpose of exciting debates, and feeling the pulse of the members, who before this had very seldom touched upon subjects of that kind.

Besides being kept busy with the routine business of our work-office, I was often engaged in executing wood-cuts for publishers and printers, at various times from about the year 1788 to 1790. The first of any importance was the wood-cuts of Roman altars, and the arms of the Bishops of Durham, for Hutchinson's *History of Durham*, in which my friend, the late George Allan, Esq., of the Grange, Darlington, took a conspicuous part. A set of cuts was done for Goldsmith's *Deserted Village*, for Mr Walker, printer of Hereford. Mr Nicholson, printer of Ludlow and Poughnill, the publishers of *Elegant Selections from Various Authors*, employed me to embellish some of these with wood-cuts. My old friend, Mr Bulmer, of the Shakespeare Printing Office, London, also employed me to execute the cuts for Parnell's *Hermit* and Goldsmith's *Deserted Village*. Many other cuts were done, from time to time, for printers in various parts of the kingdom. These formed an almost endless variety. I engraved a series of copper plates, at a low rate, for Sir Harry Liddell's and Captain Consett's *Tour to Lapland*, in 1786. My partner and self were busily engaged about the year 1796 in engraving the plan of the projected Canal from Newcastle to Carlisle for Mr Dodd the Engineer, and plans of the Estates and views of the Mansion House for a few Gentlemen who opposed the line of the Canal on the north side of the Tyne, as projected by Mr Chapman the engineer. After a great deal of scheming and manoeuvring, under the management of Raph Heron, an attorney of great ability, the whole of this great, this important national as well as local undertaking was baffled and set aside. Most men of discernment were of opinion that the coalowners 'below bridge' were the cause of it. The canal, as projected by Mr Dodd, in 1795, would have certainly opened out a territory of coal that might have affected their interest. It would appear, at least, that they dreaded it; and in this, as in almost every other case, private interest was found to overpower public good.

CHAPTER XII

HAVING, from the time that I was a schoolboy, been displeased with most of the figures in children's books, and particularly with those of the *Three Hundred Animals*, the figures in which, even at that time, I thought I could depicture much better; and having afterwards very often turned the matter over in my mind, of making improvements in that publication—I at last came to the determination of making the attempt. The extreme interest I had always felt in the hope of administering to the pleasure and amusement of youth, and judging from the feelings I had experienced myself that they would be affected in the same way as I had been, whetted me up and stimulated me to proceed. In this, my only reward besides was the great pleasure I felt in imitating nature. That I should ever do anything to attract the notice of the world, in the manner that has been done, was the farthest thing in my thoughts, and so far as I was concerned myself at that time, I minded little about any self-interested considerations. These intentions I communicated to my partner; and, though he did not doubt of my being able to succeed, yet, being a prudent, cautious, and thinking man, he wished to be more satisfied as to the probability of such a publication paying for the labour. On this occasion, being little acquainted with the nature of such undertakings, we consulted our friend Solomon Hodgson, bookseller and editor of the *Newcastle Chronicle*, as to the probability of its success, etc., when he most warmly encouraged us to proceed.

Such animals as I knew, I drew from memory on the wood; others which I did not know were copied from Dr Smellie's* *Abridgement of Buffon*, and other naturalists, and also from the animals which were from time to time exhibited in shows. Of these last, I made sketches first from memory, and then corrected and finished the drawings upon the wood from a second examination of the different animals. I began this business of cutting the blocks with the figure of the dromedary, on the 15th November 1785, the day on which my father died. I then proceeded in copying such figures as above named as I did not hope to see alive. The figures which were done from nature or from memory, so much attracted the notice of our friend that he ardently insisted upon our making our work assume a superior character to that of the 'shabby book' we had only been thinking of surpassing; and from the opinion we had formed of his being better acquainted with business than we were, we offered him a third share, free from any expense for the cuts. A proper agreement was made, and he became our partner in the *History of Quadrupeds*. While I was busied in drawing and cutting the figures of animals, and also in designing and engraving the vignettes, Mr Beilby, being of a bookish or reading turn, proposed, in his evenings at home, to write or compile the descriptions, but not knowing much about natural history we got books on that subject to enable him to form a better notion of these matters. With this I had little more to do than furnishing him, in many conversations and

* [William Smellie (1740–95), Edinburgh printer, naturalist, and antiquary.]

121

by written memoranda, with what I knew of animals, and blotting out, in his manuscript, what was not truth. In this way we proceeded till the book was published in 1790.

It is worthy of remark that while the title-page was in hand, Mr Beilby wished to be made the author of it, and wrote in his name as such 'by R. Beilby'. On Mr Hodgson seeing this, without saying a word he stroked the name out with a pen, while Mr Beilby was looking on. I knew nothing of this transaction for some time afterwards, and it might have passed so, for anything I cared about the authorship, or whose name was put to it as such. It was sufficient for me that I had the opportunity of giving vent to my feelings and gratifying my desires in doing my part of the work. The greater part of these wood-cuts were drawn and engraved at night, after the day's work of the shop was over. In these evenings, I frequently had the company of my friend the Rev Richard Oliphant, who took great pleasure in seeing me work, and who occasionally read to me the sermons he had composed for the next Sunday. I was also often attended, from a similar curiosity, by my friend, the Rev Thomas Hornby, lecturer at St John's Church. He would not, like my friend Oliphant, adjourn to a public-house, and join in a tankard of ale, but he had it sent for to my workplace. We frequently disagreed in our opinions as to religious matters, he being, as I thought, an intolerant, high churchman; but, notwithstanding this, he was a warm well-wisher and kind friend, and was besides of so charitable a disposition that his purse was ever open to relieve distress, and he would occasionally commission me to dispose of a guinea anonymously to persons in want.

As soon as the *History of Quadrupeds* appeared, I was surprised to find how rapidly it sold. Several other editions quickly followed, and a glut of praises was bestowed upon the book. The first time I was obliged to hear personal praises, on this account, was from Dr David Ure, LL.D, of Glasgow, who called to see me, and not being used to such compliments, I blushed over the ears, and left him talking to Mr Beilby. These and such like praises, however, excited envy, and were visibly followed by the balance of an opposite feeling from many people at home; for they raked together, and blew up, the embers of envy into a transient blaze; but the motives by which I was actuated stood out of the reach of its sparks, and they returned into the heap whence they came, and fell into dust. I was much more afraid to meet the praises which were gathered around than I was of the sneers which they excited; and poetry appeared in the paper, I was obliged on its account, for some time, to shun 'Swarley's Club', of which the writer, George Byles, was a member, to avoid the warm and sincere compliments that awaited me there.

I had long made up my mind not to marry whilst my father and mother lived, in order that my undivided attention might be bestowed upon them. My mother had, indeed, recommended a young person in the neighbourhood to me as a wife. She did not know the young lady intimately, but she knew she was modest in her deportment, handsome in her person, and had a good fortune; and, in compliance with this recommendatiom, I got acquainted with her, but was careful not to proceed further, and soon discovered that, though her character was innocence itself, she was mentally one of the weakest of her sex. The smirking lasses of Tyneside had long thrown out their jibes against me, as being a woman-hater, but in this they were greatly mistaken. I had, certainly, been very guarded in my conduct towards them, as I held it extremely wrong and cruel to sport with the feelings of any one in making them believe that I was in love with any of them without really being so. In this, which was one of my resolves, sincerity and truth were my guides. As I ever considered a matrimonial connection as a business of the utmost importance, and which was to last till death made the separation, while looking about for a partner for life, my anxious attention was directed to the subject. I had long considered it to be the duty of every man (in health), on changing his life, to get a healthy woman for his wife, for the sake of his children, and a sensible one, as a companion, for his own happiness and comfort—that love is the natural guide in this business, and much misery is its attendant when that is wanting. This being the fixed state of my mind, I permitted no mercenary considerations to interfere. Impressed with these sentiments, I had long, my dear Jane, looked upon your mother as a suitable helpmate for me. I had seen her in prosperity and in adversity; and in the latter state she appeared to me to the greatest advantage. In this she soared above her sex, and my determination was fixed. In due time we were married, and from that day to this no cloud, as far as concerned ourselves, has passed over us, to obscure a life-time of uninterrupted happiness.

During the time I was busied with the figures of the *History of Quadrupeds*, many jobs interfered to cause delay; one of which was the wood-cut of the Chillingham wild bull, for the late Marmaduke Tunstal, Esq., of Wycliffe. This very worthy gentleman and good naturalist honoured me with his approbation of what I had done, and was one of our correspondents. He, or my friend, George Allan, Esq., employed me to undertake this job; and on Easter Sunday 1789, I set off on foot to Chillingham, accompanied by my acquaintance, William Preston, the printer, on this business. After tarrying a little with friends at Morpeth and Alnwick, we took Huln Abbey on our way across the country to the place of our destination. Besides seeing the various kinds of pheasants, etc., at the last-named place, little occurred to attract attention, except our being surrounded, or beset, in passing over a moor, by burning heather, and afterwards passing over the surface of immense old winter wreaths of frozen snow. Arrived at Chillingham, we took up our abode with my kind old friend John Bailey, and spent a cheerful evening with him after our fatigue. Next day, Mr B. accompanied me to the park, for the purpose of seeing the wild cattle. This, however, did not answer my purpose; for I could make no drawing of the bull, while he, along with the rest of the herd, was wheeling about, and then fronting us, in the manner described in the *History of Quadrupeds.* I was therefore obliged to endeavour to see one which had been conquered by his rival, and driven to seek shelter alone, in the quarry-holes or in the woods; and, in order to get a good look at one of this descriptiom, I was under the necessity of creeping on my hands and knees, to leeward, and out of his sight; and I thus got my sketch or memorandum, from which I made my drawing on the wood. I was sorry my figure was made from one before he was furnished with his curled or shaggy neck and mane.

On our return home, my companion and I took up our abode for two days and nights, at Eslington, in the apartments of our kind and hearty friend, John Bell, then steward to Sir Harry Liddell, Bart., and afterwards a merchant at Alnmouth. Having made a drawing from the large Newfoundland dog kept there, and rambled about visiting some of Mr Bell's friends, we then bent our way homewards, highly satisfied with the journey, crowned as it was with hospitality and kindness which could not be surpassed.

In the year 1790, I was employed much in the same way as I had been in other years about that period; but this was besides marked by an event which enwrapped and dwelt on my mind. No doubt all thinking men in their passage through life must have had similar experiences. My old and revered preceptor, the Rev Christopher Gregson, died this year. No sooner did the news of his extreme illness reach me, than I set off, in my usual way, and with all speed, to Ovingham. I instantly entered his room, and there I found his niece, Miss Dinah Bell (afterwards Mrs Johnson), in close attendance upon him. With her, being intimately acquainted, I used no ceremony, but pulled the curtain aside, and then beheld my friend, in his last moments. He gave me his last look, but could not speak. Multitudinous reflections of things that were passed away, hurried on my mind, and these overpowered me. I knew not what to say, except 'Farewell for ever! farewell!' Few men have passed away on Tyneside so much respected as Mr Gregson. When he was appointed to the curacy of Ovingham, I understand his income was not more than thirty pounds per annum. Thus set down, he began by taking pupils to board and educate, chiefly as Latin scholars; and Mrs Gregson (late Miss Longstaff), after my mother left him, did everything in her power to make the seminary respectable. He afterwards, however, commenced teaching on a more extended scale, by taking in scholars of all kinds, from their A, B, C's, to the classics. In this, his task must have been of the most arduous description, which he got through without any usher or assistant. His assiduity must have attracted the notice of the late Thomas Charles Bigge, Esq., of Benton, the lay rector, for he added some land to the glebe, by way of bettering his condition. Little as this farm was, as to its magnitude, it enabled him, by his good management and unceasing industry, to show himself a good farmer, and he was not a little vain on being complimented on this score. As a clergyman, he was not one of the fittest for that very important office; but this was chiefly owing to his defective voice, which was so low and raucous, that his hearers could not so well profit by his sensible discourses. In another way—I mean as a village lawyer— he stood pre-eminent. His pen was ever ready at the service of his parishioners, and whatever dispute arose amongst them there was never any objection to leave the matter to the decision of Mr Gregson; and I have often heard it asserted that there was not one lawsuit in the parish while he was minister there. He set out in life on this poor curacy, upon a system of great economy, and perhaps, like other frugal people, it grew upon him till he was accused of 'nearness'; but, be this as it may, he accumulated, after a life of great good management, a sum of about nine hundred pounds. If his pen was ever ready to serve his parishioners, so, on certain occasions was his purse; for he eyed with great attention the situation of such of his neighbours as were industrious; and, when he found these were struggling under untoward circumstances, or unforeseen losses, without being solicited, he lent them money to ward off the evil, and to serve their need.

The publication of the *Quadrupeds* led me into a close intimacy with Solomon Hodgson, and others of his friends, and also with other men of distinguished abilities, with Andrew Young, MD, Samuel Burton Pearson, MD, and Nathan Surgeon, surgeon. These men were eminent in their professions, and were besides of charitable, humane and noble dispositions, and it is equally true and distressing to think that tho' nature had done everything for them, they, as it were, threw her favours in her face and all fell victims to the Bottle. With this company and their conversations I often felt much pleased, but it sometimes led me to join with them in their excesses. There were also others with whom I occasionally spent my evenings over a cheerful glass in their agreeable company, viz., the Revd. John Hogarth (afterwards Rector of Kirknewton), my friend the Revd. Richard Oliphant, John Stokoe, architect, and John Howard, the author of a work on Spherical Geometry. To enumerate one half of the people with whom I was acquainted would swell the list to an extent that might be wearisome to read over; but I may venture to name a few with whom I was in habits of intimacy, and who also stood

127

pre-eminent on account of their great worth, and the estimation in which they were held by the public. Among the first was William Charnley, bookseller. This intelligent and honest man, I account as one of the Newcastle worthies. The Revd. William Turner,* Secretary to the Literary and Philosophical Society in Newcastle, and Minister of the Unitarian Chapel. He was in my way of judging a Master of Arts. His talents were great in various departments of science and as a lecturer on such subjects, and I know not how I can say more or less of him than that his character was composed of everything great, good, amiable and praiseworthy. His friend and associate, Robert Doubleday, vice-president of the Literary and Philosophical Society, also partook very greatly of the same good qualities and attainments as Mr Turner. There were others, set after set, with whom I lived in habits of intimacy, and some of these may be dated a long way back. Gilfrid Ward, woollen draper (of facetious memory); he died 25th of January 1798, aged 52 years, and was buried at St John's; Joseph Bell, painter, he also displayed considerable abilities as a painter, poet, and a man of talents in other respects, but with keeping much company, he became also much dissipated; he died 26th April 1806, aged 60, and was buried at St Andrews. I was also long acquainted with William Bell, portrait painter, etc. He was, as a painter, accounted eminent in that profession, and was awarded a gold medal from the Society of Arts for the best historical painting. He died in Newcastle Infirmary in the year 1830, aged 60. I was also long afterwards on the most friendly terms with James Ramsey, the very eminent portrait painter. Another worthy with whom I spent many a pleasant evening was William Gill. He had long been colliery agent to Lord Windsor (one of the partners of the Grand Allies) in which office he was much esteemed. He

* [1761–1859.]

was a man of great reading, and had reflected upon what he read. He was also, like all men of sense and spirit, of a patriotic turn, and foretold the consequences of the late war of Kings, which he considered as an attempt to destroy the civil liberties of mankind; and I have often since wondered to find his predictions unfold themselves so truly as they have done. In this he was simple, plain and argumentative, and they were dictated only by truth and sincerity. He was of a social turn of mind, and for an old man was wonderfully clear, sensible and cheerful, and this prompted him to select such as he thought were of the same stamp, and these he often invited to spend the evening with him. He also besides these pleasing qualities was an attentively judicious and charitable man, and in this way did not do that business by halves, for wherever he found an honest industrious man with a family, struggling to get forward, he never lost sight of him until he placed him in a fair way to prosperity. He however outlived his faculties and left all his property past his poor relations, particularly a brother who was a poor schoolmaster, but who I believe he was persuaded was dead, as well as others of his near relations whom he once intended to provide for.

CHAPTER XIII

WHILE the sale of edition after edition of the *Quadrupeds* was going on with great success, I turned my thoughts to the *History of British Birds*. I felt greatly charmed with, and had long paid great attention to, the subject; and I had busied myself very much in reading various works. As far as I can now recollect, the first books I had become acquainted with were Brookes' and Miller's *Natural History*, and Dr Smellie's *Abridgement of Buffon*. These were now thrown, as it were, into the background; having been succeeded by Pennant's works. I might name others I had perused, chiefly lent to me by my kind friend George Allan, Esq. These consisted of Albin's *History of Birds*, Belon's very old book, Willoughby and Ray,* etc. Mr John Rotherham gave me *Gesner's Natural History*. With

---

* Francis Willughby's *Ornithology* (1678) in Ray's edition.

some of these I was in raptures. Willoughby and Ray struck me as having led the way to truth, and to British ornithology. The late Michael Bryan, Esq., of London, formerly of Newcastle, lent me the splendid volumes, *Planches Enluminées*, of Buffon, and George Silvertop, Esq., of Minsteracres, *Edwards's Natural History*. I was much pleased with White's *History of Selborne*. Pennant, however, opened out the largest field of information and on his works I bestowed the most attention. Latham seems to have wound up the whole, and I have often lamented that it was not—by being embellished with correct figures—made a great national work, like the Count de Buffon's. The last of our ornithologists, and one of the most indefatigable, was the late Col George Montagu, author of the *Ornithological Dictionary*.

As soon as it was spread abroad that we were engaged with the *History of Birds and their Figures*, I was in consequence led into a seemingly endless correspondence with friends and amateurs; so much so, that I often felt myself unable duly to acknowledge the obligations I owed them, and many a letter I have written after so being wearied out with the labours of the day, that I often forgot how to spell the commonest words, and I fear the rest of many of my letters would be a piece with this—and not clear nor very intelligible.

At the beginning of this undertaking I made up my mind to copy nothing from the works of others, but to stick to nature as closely as I could; and for this purpose, being invited by Mr Constable, the then owner of Wycliffe, I visited the extensive museum there, collected by the late Marmaduke Tunstal, Esq., to make drawings of the birds. I set off from Newcastle on the 16th July 1791, the day on which my friend Dr Bailes died, and remained at the above beautiful place nearly two months, drawing from the stuffed specimens. I lodged in the house of John Goundry, the person who preserved the birds for Mr Tunstal; and boarded at his father's, George Goundry, the old miller there. Whilst I remained at Wycliffe, I frequently dined with the Rev Thomas Zouch, the rector of the parish. He watched my going out of church on the Sundays, where I often attended, accompanied by old Goundry, to invite me to dine with him. On these occasions he often made the character of his late neighbour, Mr Tunstal, and of George Goundry, the subject of his conversation, and dwelt with great pleasure on the excellence of both. Mr Tunstal was a Roman Catholic, and had a chapel in his own house; Mr Zouch was a Church of England minister; and George Goundry was a Deist; and yet these three uncommonly good men, as neighbours, lived in constant charity and goodwill towards each other. Mr Zouch would sometimes say to me, 'Do you know this old man can beat me in argument', and would then regret that he was not orthodox in his religious opinions, but setting that aside, as to his moral conduct, he was one of the best Christians he knew. Poor Goundry was equally warm in his praises of these two good men his neighbours, and with the tear on his cheek would enumerate the charities and liberality of the late Mr Tunstal, and as a proof of the latter he instanced his being at great expense in privately contributing towards the pewing of Wycliffe Church. One might dwell long with pleasure on such singularly good characters. I wish the world was better stocked with them.

On my return from Wycliffe, being thoroughly drenched with an incessant rain, I called upon an old and much-esteemed schoolfellow, John Forster, at Bishop Auckland, and spent a day or two with him, in busy converse about our former transactions at school, etc. Perhaps few have passed through life without experiencing the pleasure that a retrospect of the times gone by thus afford to old cronies, in tailing over the recollections of youthful frolics, and

132

even of the discipline which followed in consequence of them.

As soon as I arrived in Newcastle, I immediately began to engrave from the drawings of the birds I had made at Wycliffe; but I had not been long thus engaged till I found the very great difference between preserved specimens and those from Nature; no regard having been paid, at that time, to fix the former in their proper attitudes, nor to place the different series of the feathers so as to fall properly upon each other. It has always given me a great deal of trouble to get at the markings of the dishevelled plumage; and, when done with every pains, I never felt satisfied with them. I was on this account driven to wait for birds newly shot, or brought to me alive, and in the intervals employed my time in designing and engraving tailpieces, or vignettes. My sporting friends, however, supplied me with birds as fast as they could; but none more so than my kind friend the late Major H. F. Gibson, of the 4th Dragoons. Lieut-Col Dalton, Major Shore, Captain (now General) Dalbiac, and other officers of the same regiment, also showed great attention to our growing work. George Strickland, Esq., of Ripon, also interested himself in his contributions for the same work. Besides these, many birds were sent to me by friends from various parts of the Kingdom, but the obligations I owe are mostly acknowledged in their proper place in the work. After working many a late hour upon the cuts, the first volume of the book was at length finished at press in September 1797. Our friend Solomon Hodgson had no share with us in this work. Mr Beilby undertook the writing or compilation of this (the first) volume, in which I assisted him a great deal more than I had done with the *Quadrupeds*. I was however surprised to find that in an Introduction written by him he took occasion to bestow the most unqualified praises on me for the assistance I had given him, by which I found he was this time determined upon being an author. I only observed that I thought the *Quadrupeds*, with the title of 'Beilby and Bewick' as the Editors, had done very well, and I could see no reason for making any change. I found Mr Beilby had imparted his ideas of becoming author to the Revd. Thomas Hornby, while the latter was at supper with him, as indeed he often was, when Mr Hornby took

occasion to express his opinion of this business, and to advise him not to think upon doing any such thing, observing that he would have written a History of Birds for me, and that some of the Doctors I was so intimate with, would with pleasure have done the same, perhaps better than he could have done it, but that in neither case could they have hoped to sell a single edition without my cuts. After Mr Hornby had slept and turned the business over in his mind, he called upon me, and with a kind of indignant feeling advised me not to permit any such thing. Other friends also did the same, and used the same kind of reasoning. In this unsettled state of affairs, Mr and Mrs Beilby set off in the pet, upon a visit to Mr Wilkinson's at Sleekburn, where they remained about a fortnight. On Mr Beilby's return I asked him if he still persisted in being named as the author of the book, to which he replied in the affirmative. 'Then, Sir,' said I, 'if you can point out a single sentence from one end of this volume of the *History of Birds* to the other of original matter as your own, I shall be glad to see it.' At this he hesitated. I then proposed to him to leave the discussion as to the authorship to our mutual friends, who knew everything relative to the matter in dispute between us, adding that if they agreed in thinking that he ought to be 'the author', it should be so, and that I never would say a word more about it. To this he agreed, and as the work was at a stand, no time was to be lost, after naming our referees. Mr Charnley, the Revd. Wm. Turner, Mr Sol. Hodgson, and Mr Robert Doubleday were instantly for that purpose summoned to meet that afternoon. We both guessed, without saying a word to each other, that Mr Charnley would be fixed on as President; and he being very deaf, we each of us, without mentioning our intentions, stated our separate cases in writing directed to him. As soon as he and his colleagues had read Mr Beilby's he handed it to me, and I read it. Mine was next given to Mr C., who, in like manner, showed it to the others, and then gave it to Mr Beilby, but he declined looking at it, and it was given to me again. After this we were desired to retire, when they committed what they had agreed upon to writing, the whole of which was printed in the concluding part of the preface to the first volume of the *Birds*, and so the matter was left without naming either him or myself as authors of the work, otherwise than as before, and of the wood-cuts being acknowledged as my

135

own. After this, Mr Beilby gave up the engraving business, and dedicated his whole time to the watch-crystal and clock manufactory, in which he had been long engaged before our separation.

The printing of other editions of the first volume of the *Birds* still met with a ready sale; but some disputes happening between us and Mrs Hodgson, the widow of our much esteemed friend, respecting the printing of the *Quadrupeds*, Mr Beilby, who now sought repose, and could not be turmoiled with disputes of any kind, sold me his third share of that publication. Sometime before the second volume of the *Birds* was put to press, he also sold me his share of this first volume. For his third share of the *Quadrupeds* I paid him one hundred pounds, and for his half share of the first volume of the *Birds* I paid him three hundred pounds. I had no sooner agreed to give this latter sum than many recollections of the past crowded upon my mind, and looking at the unfavourable side, I could not help thinking of the extra labour and time I had spent in the completion of these works, wherein he had borne comparatively a small part—nor even an equivalent as to his time and labour in the other department of our business; and in this instance I could not help thinking that he had forgot himself and had suffered greediness to take possession of his mind; but, having promised to pay the sum, I made no further observations to any one. On the other side of this account, I called to my remembrance the many obligations I owed him, for the wise admonitions he had given, and the example he had set me, while I was only a wild and giddy youth. These I never could forget, and they implanted so rooted a respect for him that I had grudged nothing I could do to promote his happiness. I had noticed, for some time past, that he had been led under a guidance and influence that made an alteration in his conduct and character for the worse; and he appeared to me not to be the Ralph Beilby* he had been, for before this, he deservedly bore the character of being a sensible judicious fair-dealing industrious man, and a good member of society. I used always to think him careful and sometimes penurious, and this disposition might indeed have crept and increased upon him; but, whatever natural failings might be in his composition, these had heretofore been checked and regulated by the rules of morality and religion. It seemed to me that it must have been a maxim with him to do justice to all, but not to confer favours upon any one; and yet he often joined me in conferring such, in various ways, upon our apprentices and others of our workpeople, for which we commonly had dirt thrown in our faces.

It does not require any great stretch of observation to discover that gratitude is a rare virtue, and that, whatever favours are poured upon an ungrateful man, he will conclude that these would not have been bestowed upon him had he not deserved them. In these our gifts to prentices and others of that stamp, I was to blame in thus conferring favours that it would have been as well to let alone. In other charities he was not backward in contributing his mite, but in these matters he was led by wisdom. In the former case, mine, by giving vent to my feelings, were led by folly; but, indeed, these follies were trivial compared with others relative to money matters, in which I had been led away by my feelings, in lending money to some, and in being bound for the payment of it for others, which, if I had been more of his disposition, would not have happened; and I now clearly see and feel that, had it not been for these imprudences, I should at this day, have found myself in better and very different circumstances than those I am in. My partner, indeed, often watched, and sometimes prevented me, from engaging in such ruinous concerns, and

* Ralph Beilby, engraver, Newcastle, died 4th Jan., 1817, aged 73, and was buried at St Andrew's.

137

would remark to me that it was impossible to serve any man who would not serve himself. After Mr Beilby was done with any concern in the publications, I found I could not go on pleasantly with Mrs Hodgson in the printing of the *Quadrupeds*, and I therefore offered either to buy her share or sell her mine, but this she declined doing, and sometime after this, she sold hers to Messrs Longman & Co, London, and since that time, the publication, shared in this way, has gone on between us.

As soon as Mr Beilby left me, I was obliged, from necessity, not choice, to commence author. As soon as each bird was finished on the wood, I set about describing it from my specimen, and at the same time consulted every authority I could meet with, to know what had been said; and this, together with what I knew from my own knowledge, were then compared; and, in this way, I finished as truly as I could the second volume of the *History of British Birds*. I also examined the first volume, with a view to correct its errors, and to add many new figures and descriptions of them to it. Although all this could not be done but by close, and, indeed, severe confinement and application, yet I was supported by the extreme pleasure I felt in depicturing and describing these beautiful and interesting aerial wanderers of the British Isles. I also hoped that my labours might perhaps have the effect of inveigling my youthful countrymen to be smitten with the charms which this branch—and, indeed, every other department of Natural History—imparts, and with the endless pleasures afforded to all who wish to 'trace Nature up to Nature's God'.

While I was thus proceeding, I was countenanced, encouraged and flattered by amateurs, who took a deep interest in my growing work, and seemed to partake the ardour in which I had long indulged. From them birds were sent to me from far and near; but to give a list of the names of these friends, and to detail the kindness I experienced first and last, might indeed be giving vent to my feelings of gratitude, but it would far exceed the bounds prescribed to this Memoir.

CHAPTER XIV

WHILST I was engaged with figures of the Water-Birds, and the Vignettes, and writing the *History*, I was greatly retarded by being obliged often to lay that work aside, to do various other jobs in the wood engraving, also the work of the shop, for my customers in the town, particularly writing engraving, which, I may say, I was obliged to learn and to pursue after Mr Beilby left me. The most interesting part of this kind of work was plates for bank-notes, cheques, etc.; but, as one of the most important of these was a five pound note for the Carlisle Bank, which attracted much notice, it may be right to give some account of it. It happened, one evening, that, whilst I was in company with George Losh, Esq., who was in some way connected with that bank, he asked me if I could engrave a bank-note that could not be easily forged. In reply, I told him I thought I could. 'Then,' said he, 'do it immediately'; and I lost no time in beginning upon it. I had, at that time, never seen a ruling machine, nor the beautiful engine-turning lately brought into use by Perkins, Fairman, and

Heath, which was at that time, I believe, utterly unknown. I however, proceeded with my plate, and my object was to make the device look like a wood-cut; and in this, though a first attempt, I succeeded; and the number of impressions wanted were sent to Carlisle.

Soon after this, I was told by Sir T[homas] F[rankland], Bart., that his brother, who held some office under government, and was much with the King—George III, whose curiosity was insatiable as to everything relative to the arts—had got one of these bank-notes. Sir T. F[rankland]'s brother showed it to the King, who greatly admired and approved of it. About two years after this, in the year 1801, Samuel Thornton, Esq., of the Bank of England, wrote to me respecting this note, and wished to know how it was executed, and whether it was done on wood or copper, etc. I was strongly advised, by a friend, not to give the gentlemen of that bank any information whatever about my plate; 'for,' said he, 'as soon as they know the nature of what they are enquiring after, you will hear no more from them'. I did not take his advice; and, after a deal of trouble in writing to them, and stating amongst many other matters that, 'though my plate would do well for country banks, it would not do for the great number wanted for the Bank of England', the business ended in nothing. It may perhaps be well, while I am on the subject of bank-notes, to pass over a number of years, and come down to the year 1818, when a commission was appointed to investigate the business of forgery, and to endeavour to prevent it in future. Some time previous to this, I was employed by my friend, John Bailey, Esq., of Chillingham, to engrave plates to prevent a repetition of the pen-and-ink forgeries which had been committed upon the Berwick Bank, which it was found had been better imitations than could be made from copper plates. In this I succeeded; and also, by a simple process, on the plates I engraved for the Northumberland Bank. Immediately on the heel of this, and as soon as the commissioners above-mentioned had commenced their enquiries, it seemed as if the services and abilities of all the artists in the kingdom were held in requisition, to give in their specimens and their schemes for this purpose; and, willing to contribute all in my power to accomplish so desirable an end, I, amongst many others, gave in my plan. The leading object with me was permanency, or, in other words, to aim at executing a device that would *never* need either alteration or repairs; and the other part of my plan was, that the device should be of such a nature, that all men of common discernment could easily recognize the note as a legitimate one. In my letters to Sir Joseph Banks, I did not mention anything about using types, or how highly I approved of their use, because I knew that others had done so before, and to point out in which way I conceived they would be of importance would now be useless; since the commissioners, or the Bank, have rejected every scheme (so far as I know) that has been laid before them. This to me has always appeared strange; as, in my opinion, there have been several specimens laid before them very efficient for the purpose of preventing forgeries, if not for setting that nefarious work at rest.

The beautiful specimens first produced by Fairman, Perkins, and Heath, from their steel plates or blocks, were, in my opinion, inimitable, and quite sufficient to answer the end intended; and those afterwards brought forward, under the auspices of Sir William Congreve, are nearly of the same character and import. If an engine turner cannot set his lathe, so as to trace or copy the delicate and truly exact curves, lines, etc., which are shown in both, it is not likely that any forgery would ever be attempted upon either of them. If they had been less complex, I should have liked them better; but, as they are, the best engravers on either copper, steel, or wood, will not attempt an imitation. They may, indeed, gaze at them—*but that is all.*

It was always surprising to me that none of the ingenious schemes—so long under the consideration of the commissioners—were adopted; but, when I read, in a newspaper, that Mr Pierce had stood up in the House of Commons, and in answer to a question put to him there, had said, in reply, 'that the commissioners were of opinion that *nothing better than the old bank-note could be devised to prevent forgery*'!—then, indeed, I could scarcely believe my own eyes—my astonishment was complete, and my opinion of the whole business of this 'mountain in labour' was fixed.

During the time that the business of the commissioners seemed to me to be hanging in suspense, I wrote a letter to Sir Joseph Banks, in which I endeavoured to press upon his attention, and that of his colleagues, as a means of preventing forgery, the necessity of having the blank paper for country bank-notes printed with a new device in lieu of the little duty stamp then used, and which had simply in view the collection of the government duty. Some time after this, a long account of the inventions of Sir William Congreve, Bart., were published in the *Repository of Arts* for March 1822, setting forth how much country banks, and the whole country was obliged to him, as the inventor of, or the person who first suggested a scheme so essentially important as this for preventing forgery. As soon as I read this, I answered it in the *Monthly Magazine* of May 1822, in which I quoted my letters to the commissioners, with the dates bearing upon this very subject, and claimed for myself the merit of having first suggested the scheme. At the same time, I only requested Sir William Congreve would, on the word of a gentleman, say whether or not the scheme was his or mine. Of this neither Sir William nor any of the commissioners took any notice, excepting, indeed, something *purporting to an answer* to what I had said, by a person in the employ of Sir William, as an artist, which, though it begun very impudently, did not answer my letter at all. This I could not help treating with contempt. To enter in to a paper war with such a person, I thought would be great folly. Sir William appears to be going on prosperously, by furnishing bankers with his stamped note-papers, and printing them in the way above described.

Sir William Congreve, as a commissioner, had the advantage of seeing the various devices, and of knowing the opinions of the various artists upon these devices, which enabled him to cull and select such as appeared to him best calculated to prevent forgery; and, I think, as he was no artist himself, he should not have taken the credit either of inventor or executor of any of these devices, nor have turned the profit arising from them to his own private account. Long before the commissioners were appointed to investigate the business of forgeries, I got engaged in another work on my own account.

CHAPTER XV

DURING a severe illness with which I was visited in April
1812, brought on by a violent perspiration suddenly
checked—the particulars of which I need not detail to my
dear Jane, as the part you and your mother and sisters
took, in nursing me night and day, for so long a time, must
be fresh in all your memories, I determined, if I recovered,
to go on with a publication of *Aesop's Fables*. While I lay
helpless, from weakness, and pined to a skeleton, without
any hopes of recovery being entertained either by myself
or anyone else, I became, as it were, all mind and memory.
I readily had presented to my recollection almost everything that had passed, through life, both of what I had done
and what I had left undone. After much debating in my own
mind where I should be buried, I fixed upon Ovingham;
and, when this was settled, I became quite resigned to the
will of Omnipotence, and felt happy. I could not, however,
help regretting that I had not published a book similar to
Croxall's *Aesop's Fables*, as I had always intended to do.
I was extremely fond of that book; and, as it had afforded
me much pleasure, I thought, with better executed designs,

it would impart the same kind of delight to others that I had experienced from attentively reading it. I was also of opinion, that it had (while admiring the cuts) led hundreds of young men into the paths of wisdom and rectitude, and in that way had done more good than the pulpit.

As soon as I was so far recovered as to be able to sit at the window at home, I began to draw designs upon the wood of the fables and vignettes; and to me this was a most delightful task. In impatiently pushing forward to get to press with the publication, I availed myself of the help of my pupils—my son, William Harvey, and William Temple—who were also eager to do their utmost to forward me in the engraving business, and in my struggles to get the book ushered into the world. Notwithstanding the pleasurable business of bringing out this publication, I felt it an arduous undertaking. The execution of the fine work of the cuts, during daylight, was very trying to the eyes, and the compiling or writing the book by candlelight, in my evenings at home, together injured the optic nerve, and that put all the rest of the nerves 'out of tune'; so that I was obliged, for a short time, to leave off such intense application until I somewhat recovered the proper tone of memory and of sight. Indeed I found in this book more difficulties to conquer than I had experienced with either the *Quadrupeds* or the *Birds*. The work was finished at press on the 1st of October 1818, and was not so well printed as I expected and wished, the ink for such fine work being much too strong, black and thick. I am pleased to find the second edition, December 1823, better printed and managed.

During the eventful period of the French Revolution, and the wide-spreading war which followed in consequence of it, and in which our government became deeply engaged, extending from 1793 to 1814—a time of blood and slaughter—I frequently, by way of unbending the mind after the labours of the day, spent my evenings chiefly at the Blue Bell, in company with a set of staunch advocates for the liberties of mankind, who discussed the passing events mostly with the cool, sensible, and deliberate attention which the importance of the subject required. I have already before named some of these acquaintances to which I may now add some others, forming altogether a miscellaneous group, but over whom some men of sense and consequence in Newcastle who were commonly of the party, and from their superior attainments seemed to preside to set the example of propriety of conduct to those of a more violent turn of mind; but indeed the political enormities of the times excited the indignation of many, which it was not easy to keep within bounds. The parties which frequented the Blue Bell, and the News Room there, consisted of tradesmen, bankers' clerks, artisans, and agents of various kinds. But those with whom I particularly associated there were Ralph Crawford, shoe maker, Joseph Bulmer, builder, Phineas Crowther, founder, Michael Charlton, white smith, John Mitchell, editor of the *Tyne Mercury*, Count Raymond, French teacher and fencing master, and my more constant companion, David Sivright, gentleman. He was a man of extraordinary abilities and attainments. He belonged to an opulent family near Edinburgh, had been brought up to business in a bank there, and was afterwards a wine merchant in London, where he had associated with the highest ranks of society. I believe he failed, or at least did not prosper in business. He had been in the West Indies, and returned home in a merchant ship in company with Rodney's fleet and the French ships of war, his prizes, of which so remarkable a destruction took place in the great storm they had to encounter on their voyage to England. Whether he had been a disappointed man in the world, I know not, but to me he appeared so. He had a rooted bad opinion of most of the people in very high life, with respect to whom he might be called a misanthropist, but to others he was affable and kind, and felt most poignantly for the distresses of the unfortunate, and was ever ready to relieve them. Against the former description he appeared to me to be too violent, to the latter I think he showed something of a sickly sensibility. He could make himself extremely pleasant in company he liked, but to such as he thought badly of either as fools or knaves (and in this he was whimsical) he became quite outrageous. I think I was the last person he associated with, and even with me he often showed petulance, and as often apologized for it. He had long been used to wander about alone, and took to drinking to excess. He left Newcastle, and went to Blyth, where he died, aged 68.

I sometimes dropped in upon other parties of friends of various political opinions and attainments at Mrs Jane Elliot's at the sign of the Unicorn. These were mostly tradesmen of the genteel sort, and besides them, this house had been a kind of rendezvous or house of resort to the comedians of our theatre during the season for many years back, from the time of Heaton and Austin's Company, down to those conducted by Charles Whitlock, Jos. Munden, Stephen Kemble, etc., and still later, comprising a period of the times of Massey and Jeffries, Plat, Emery, Cook, Liston, and many others, who made a figure in their day. With Jos. Munden I often associated, and still oftener and to a later period with my friend Stephen Kemble* and his friends. In Mrs Elliot's house, and indeed in every house, politics formed the topic of conversation, and, less or more, for years back, seemed the order of the day.

In partaking in these debatings, I now find I spent rather too much time. I fear it was useless; for it requires little discernment to see that, where a man's interest is at stake, he is very unwilling to hear any argument that militates against it; and people who were well paid were

* [A brother of Mrs Siddons.]

always very loyal. To argue on any subject, unless a principle, or what mathematicians would call a datum, is first laid down to go upon, is only gabble. It begins and must end in nonsense; and I suspect that many of the long, wearisome speeches and debatings carried on for such a number of years in the Houses of Lords and Commons, as well as many of the innumerable weekly or daily essays, and some of the pamphlets which the revolution and the war gave rise to, were devoid of a right principle—a principle of rectitude to guide them. The causes of this horrid Revolution, and the equally horrible war which ended it, will form a most interesting subject for the head and pen of some future historian of a bold and enlightened mind—truly to depicture it in all its bearings, perhaps long after the animosity of party feelings and the parties themselves have died away.

From the best consideration I have been able to give to the question, I cannot help viewing it otherwise than in this way. In the year 1789, the French Revolution broke out, first of all from the income of the government not being sufficient to defray its expenditure, or in other words, from its finances having become deranged for want of money, which the people, having been taxed to the utmost and brought down to poverty, could no longer supply. The aristocracy and the priesthood (the privileged orders, as they were called) contributed little or nothing to support the state; and, instead of being the natural guardians or depositories of the honour and virtue of the nation, they were chiefly known as its oppressors. By exaction, cruelty, and tyranny, the people had long been borne down to the lowest pitch of degradation. They were considered, not as rational human beings, equal in mind and intellect to their oppressors, but as beings made for the purpose only of continually labouring to support them in all their real and imaginary wants. They were treated worse than beasts of burden, and this is nearly the case in all countries where the aristocracy are kept up and blinded by pride and guided by ignorance. In this they are supported by what may be called their satellites—a kind of bastard breed, who, in aping the worst part of the character of those exalted above them, show themselves off as the opulent, aspiring, purse-proud gentry of a country.

> 'If aught on earth th'immortal powers deride,
> 'Tis surely this,—the littleness of pride.'

This kind of treatment, so long shown to the people of France, could be endured no longer. They, indeed, seemed heartily disposed to settle a rational and just representative government quietly themselves; but this did not suit the views of the surrounding despots, to whom the very word liberty was offensive, and it was determined, at once, that this attempt of the people to resume their rights should instantly be overwhelmed. For this purpose, immense armed and well-disciplined mercenaries were gathered together, and almost surrounded the country. Thus situated and remembering the traditionary tales handed down to them of the cruelties and oppressions under which their forefathers had groaned, the French people could not bear their condition any longer. They were driven to madness, and instantly retaliated upon their oppressors, who, they conceived, meant that they and their children's children should continue to be doomed for ages to come. In this state of the public mind, the French people rose simultaneously, as one man, and with unconquerable energy and bravery, like a whirlwind, swept the advocates and the armies of despotism from off the face of the earth. Thus roused, this confederacy of Legitimates, finding or fearing that they might be baffled in their attempts, looked to England for support; and grieved, indeed, were the advocates of rational liberty to find that these enemies to freedom had not looked in vain; for the government of this free

150

country and free people—long veering, indeed, from the line of rectitude—had readily found pretexts for entering into a war in support of despotism; and war was begun, in the year 1793, against the republican government of France.

It had long been the settled opinion of many profound politicians, that corruption had spread, and was spreading, its baneful influence among the members of the government of this kingdom; and that the majority cared nothing about maintaining the constitution in its purity, which to them was become like an old song. In this state of things, with Mr Pitt at their head, and the resources of the British Isles in their hands, it was calculated upon as a certainty that his weight, added to the already powerful confederacy, would soon put a stop to the march of intellect, and, if found necessary, put an extinguisher upon the rights of man.

It is horrible to contemplate the immense destruction of human beings, and the waste of treasure, which followed and supported this superlatively wicked war. Under the mask of patriotism, Mr Pitt had begun his career, but he soon changed sides, and, blinded perhaps by ambition, became the powerful advocate of an opposite and perverted order of things. Thus situated, nothing could to a certainty serve his purpose so well as corruption; and the House of Commons had long been growing into a state befitting his purpose; for its members had, in a great degree, ceased to be the representatives of the people, and he had now only to begin an invigorated, new, or more extended system of place and patronage to have the majority at his nod; and, in aid of this, to add an extension of the peerage. This demi-oligarchy, cemented together by feelings of rapacious interests, in his hands was the best organized system of extorting money that ever had appeared in the world. They met together to tax—tax—tax; and, under various pretexts, to rob the people 'according to law', and to divide the spoil amongst themselves and their friends. Arbitrary laws were enacted, gagging bills were passed, and a system of espionage spread over the kingdom to keep the people down, many of whom seemed to have forgotten the exertions of their forefathers, whose blood has been spilt to purchase a better order of things. I felt particularly hurt at the apathy of country gentlemen in these (politically considered) worst of times. Their faculties seemed benumbed; but, indeed, most of them fell into the vortex of corruption themselves. They appeared to me to have lost their former independent character, and to be now looking out to that evil source as a provision for the younger branches of their own families, unmindful of all other ill consequences, which this selfishness blindly supported and maintained. The minions of power and spies were countenanced and protected, by which they became insolent and impudent, and walked in stately array, hand in hand, in safety. Although the friends of liberty and the constitution were both numerous and intrepid, yet, for want of what they termed respectable heads, they were widely spread and divided, and their efforts proved in vain. There was also an intermediate or neutral race, consisting of those who had not laid down any principle in politics to guide them. They were mostly such as advocated the cause of corruption; and, in listening to them, I was disgusted at their senseless arguments. They were proof against reasoning, and thoroughly convinced me that 'a wise man changes his opinion, but a fool never does'. They, however, kept on the safe side; *they were loyal*; and the gist of their arguments, with which they ended all their disputes, were summed up in this—'If you do not like your country, leave it. What do you want? are not *we* very well off?' Their reflecting powers reached no further, and they could not see by what slow degrees the arm of despotism had so often circumspectly stretched its iron hand over the liberties of the people, and then crushed them.

While bickerings and debatings were going on amongst politicians at home, the Continent was deluged with the blood of many destructive battles. The sea was also crimsoned in the same way; and it was on this element that the tide of affairs was first turned in favour of Britain, who now, by the valour of her seamen, reigned complete 'mistress of the deep', and the commerce of the world seemed to be poured into her lap. Estates rose in value to an extraordinary height, and the price of grain, etc., still more so. The shipping interest wallowed in riches; the gentry whirled about in aristocratic pomposity; they forgot what their demeanour and good, kind, behaviour used to be to those in inferior stations of life; and seemed now far too often to look upon them like dirt. The character of the farmers was also changed. They acted the gentleman very awkwardly, and could not, in these times, drink anything but wine. Even that was called 'humble port' and they were to have such kind as bore a higher price. When these upstart gentlemen left the market, they were ready to ride over all they met or overtook on the way; but this was as nothing compared to the pride and folly which took possession of their empty or fume-charged heads, when they got dressed in scarlet. They were then fitted for any purpose, and were called 'yeomanry cavalry'.* Pride and folly then became personified. When peace came, it brought with it a sudden fall in the price of corn; but the taxes continuing the same to them, and rents still keeping high, they, with few exceptions, suddenly experienced a woeful change. I cannot say, after seeing so much of their folly, that I was sorry for them; for they mostly deserved this reverse of fortune. Not so with the industrious labourer. His privations were great, and he was undeservedly doomed to

* [An obvious thrust at 'Peterloo'. Mounted yeomanry charged a crowd assembled in St Peter's Fields, Manchester, on 16 August 1819, to petition for parliamentary reform, and people were killed.]

suffer for want of employment, and often to waste away and die of hunger and want.

During the greater portion of the war, the landowners may be said to have paid little or nothing to support it; for the extra rents paid almost all their taxes; but at length the evils brought on by so long a war fell also heavily upon numbers of them, who, on account of tithes and taxes with which the land was loaded, could hardly get any rent at all.

It will seem a wonder to future ages how the British people could so long have supported the squandered expenditure of the government; still they were not like the long-worn-down subjects of continental despots; for what the latter can get from their subjects is like clippings from the back and sides of swine, while the ingenuity, the industry, and the energy of the British people furnish the well-grown fleeces of sheep. Pity it is that they should have been so often wickedly shorn to the bare skin.

The state of temporary prosperity, to which I have alluded, incited to agricultural improvements; and societies for the promotion, and premiums for the encouragement, of various desiderata blazed forth over a great part of the kingdom. Cattle, sheep, horses, and swine, all of which were called 'live stock', occupied a great deal of attention, and in the improvement of the various breeds agriculturists succeeded to a certain, and in some cases, perhaps, to a great extent. And yet I cannot help thinking that they often suffered their whimsies to overshoot the mark, and in many instances to lead them on to the ridiculous.

After all—these enquiries having opened the eyes of the landlords to their own interests—it is not unlikely that the man of industry, the plain, plodding farmer will, without receiving any reward, have to pay for these improvements. My kind, my intimate friend, John Bailey, Esq., of Chillingham, in conjunction with another friend of mine, George Culley, Esq., of Fowberry, were the active, judicious, and sensible authors of many of the agricultural reports, in which they did not lose sight of the farmer. They wished to inculcate the principle of 'to live and let live' between landlord and tenant.

It will readily be supposed, that, where such exertions were made, and pains taken to breed the best kinds of all the domestic animals, jealousy and envy would be excited, and contentions arise as to which were the best; but for me to dilate upon this would only lead me out of the way. I shall, however, notice an instance, as it happened to occur between my two friends, Mr Smith, of Woodhall, and Mr Bailey. The latter, in connection with his report on Cheviot sheep, had given a bad figure of a ram of that breed. This was construed into a design to lessen the character of Mr Smith's Cheviot sheep, on which, in April 1798, the latter sent for me to draw and engrave a figure of one of his rams, by way of contrasting it with the figure Mr Bailey had given. The colour Mr Smith gave to the business was, not to find fault with Mr Bailey's figure, but to show how much he (Mr Smith) had improved the breed since Mr Bailey had written his report.

Whilst I was at Woodhall, I was struck with the sagacity of a dog belonging to Mr Smith. The character for sagacity of the Shepherd's Dog was well-known to me, but this instance of it was exemplified before my own eyes. Mr Smith wished to have a particular ram brought out from amongst the flock, for the purpose of my seeing it. Before we set out, he observed to the shepherd, that he thought the old dog (he was grey-headed and almost deaf and blind) would do well enough for what he wanted with him. Before we reached the down, where the flock was feeding, I observed that Mr Smith was talking to the dog before he ordered him off on his errand; and, while we were conversing on some indifferent subject, the dog brought a ram before us. Mr Smith found a deal of fault with the dog, saying, Did I not order you so and so? and he scolded him for bringing a wrong sheep, and then, after fresh directions, set him off again to bring the one he wished me to see. We then returned home, and shortly after our arrival there, the dog brought the very ram wanted, along with a few other sheep, into the fold, where I took a drawing of him.

Shortly after my return from Woodhall, I was sent for to Darlington, and thence to Barmpton, to make drawings of cattle and sheep, to be engraved for a Durham report. After I had made my drawings from the fat sheep, I soon saw that they were not approved, but that they were to be made like certain paintings shown to me. I observed to my employer that the paintings bore no resemblance to the animals whose figures I had made my drawings from; and that I would not alter mine to suit the paintings that were shown to me; but, if it were wished that I should make engravings from these paintings, I had not the slightest objection to do so, and I would also endeavour to make *facsimiles* of them. This proposal would not do; and my journey, as far as concerned these fat cattle makers, ended in nothing. I objected to put lumps of fat here and there where I could not see it, at least not in so exaggerated a way as on the painting before me; so 'I got my labour for my trouble'. Many of the animals were, during this *rage* for fat cattle, fed up to as great a weight and bulk as it was possible for feeding to make them; but this was not enough; they were to be figured monstrously fat before the owners of them could be pleased. Painters were found who were quite subservient to this guidance, and nothing else would satisfy. Many of these paintings will mark the times, and, by the exaggerated productions of the artists, serve to be laughed at when the folly and the self-interested motives which gave birth to them are done away.

CHAPTER XVI

Further remarks on the measures and supporters of Mr Pitt — Witches — Their treatment — Consequences of ignorance — Mr Pitt's motives — General Bonaparte's victories — His ambition and consequent ruin — Reflections on war and its horrors — What might have been done with the men and the money — The moss-troopers — Their ferocity.

FROM this time till the peace was concluded, the political debatings, before noticed, continued, and were almost the constant subject of all companies. I have often sat and listened with wonder to the jargon of the protected fools, and heard them argue, if so it may be called, in defence of all the measures then pursued; and I have seen with surprise the impudence of those who lived upon the taxes. Knaves and their abettors appeared to predominate in the land; and they carried their subserviency to such a length that I think, if Mr Pitt had proposed to make a law to transport all men who had pug noses, and to hang all men above 60 years of age, these persons (those excepted who came within the meaning of the act) would have advocated it as a brilliant thought and a wise measure.

If we examine the history of these times, and look back to those of old, we shall find that the inroads of ignorance have ever been the same. The time was when the magistrates of Newcastle sent to Scotland for a man who was reputed clever in discovering witches. He came, and easily convicted many a fine woman, as well as those who were wrinkled by age and wisdom, and they were by his means tried and put to death.

I think, if there be a plurality of devils, ignorance must be their king. The wretchedness which ignorance has, from time to time, spread over the world is truly appalling. This is a king that should be deposed without loss of time; and that portion of mankind who are under the guidance of his imps, should have nothing to do with the affairs of society, and should be carefully looked to and kept out of every kind of command. Even the poor, innocent, unreasoning animals should, in mercy, not be allowed to be goaded, and to suffer under folly and cruelty.

To attempt giving anything like a detail of the history of this eventful war would, in this place, be useless: that must be left to the historian. It appears to me that Mr Pitt was urged into it chiefly by ambition, and that disappointment broke his heart. General Bonaparte, from his unparalleled victories, became in his turn blinded by ambition, which ended in his being conquered and banished to St Helena for life. He had divided and conquered, in victory after victory, almost all his continental enemies, one after another, and then mostly reinstated them in their dominions. But this generosity would not do. Despotism, urged on and supported by this country, was rooted too deeply in the governments of Europe to think of making any change to better the condition of the people. It would appear that that is a business they cannot think of; and the old maxim, that the many are made only to support the few, seems continually uppermost in their resolves. If Bonaparte had been as good a man as he was a great one, he had it in his power to settle all this, and to have established the happiness of both the governors and the governed, over all the civilized world, for ages to come. Although he had the example of the incomparable Washington before him, he did not copy it. He ceased to be first consul, managed to assume the title of emperor, married an Austrian archduchess, and became one of the Legitimates. This added to the stock of his ambition, and from that time he began to decline. Fortune at length seemed to frown upon him, and the frost and snow of Russia cut off and destroyed his immensely large and well-appointed army. He was baffled in his strenuous efforts to repair his loss, and his defeat at Waterloo sealed his ruin.

One would think that the gaining of worlds would not compensate for the misery and the horrid waste of human life which are the certain attendants of war; and one would wonder what kind of materials men are made of, or what kind of minds and souls direct the actions of the authors of it. Were they to reflect, it may be fairly concluded that they could not bear their own thoughts, and that, after taking a full survey of the wretchedness they had occasioned, they would go immediately and hang themselves. But it would appear that the lives of human beings weigh little in the scale of great man-killers. They are perhaps not fitted for reflection, or only for that kind of it which can look at nothing but ambition or private gain. It would be well for the abettors and advocates of war to try to weigh the profit and loss (setting aside the inhumanity) attendant upon it. This we should do at home; and, instead of celebrating the birthday of the 'Heaven-born minister', ask his admirers how he deserves such a title, and compare it with his actions. Might not the lives of, say, a million of men have been saved? Was it necessary that they should have been sacrificed in such a way? Could he have avoided it? With his consummate abilities, I humbly think he could. Would not these men have been sufficient in number to colonize and to civilize immense unoccupied territories? The money wasted would have accomplished almost anything. The men and the money would have canaled Britain and Ireland from end to end, and intersected them from side to side; and also made piers, where wanted, at the mouths of the rivers of the two islands; and, besides,

159

would have converted both countries into gardens. To point out more improvements would be a waste of words. With such means in hand, they might have been almost endless. Then, per contra: What has been done in exchange for the millions of lives and the millions of money thus spent? They have restored legitimacy; they have restored 'Louis the Desired', and 'Ferdinand the Beloved', and the Inquisition! Monarchs are still to be called 'God's vicegerents here on earth'! When by their actions they show themselves deserving of such titles, mankind will not disturb them in these their dreams; but, till then, they will continue to smile at the conceit, as well as the glitter they keep up to dazzle the sight of their purblind 'loving subjects'. All wars, except defensive ones, are detestable; and, if governments admitted morality into their institutions, and were guided by its precepts, war would, in all probability, grow into disuse, and cease. But hitherto that treasure of inestimable value, I think, has been discarded from their councils, and I cannot discover much difference between them and the lesser banditti of old; for each has been guided by the strong disposition to rob (as soon as they thought themselves able successfully to do so), and to show that 'might is right'. From the feuds of the nobility down to 'Rob-in-hood, Will Scarlet, and Little John'; and from the ferocious combats of the Percy and Douglas, on the Borders—of Johnny Armstrong and his eight score men, down to 'Yeddy (Adam) Bell', 'Clem of the Clough', and 'William of Cloudsley'—and the moss-troopers—the same wicked principle has guided them and their ferocious retainers to murder each other and to soak the earth with blood.

CHAPTER XVII

It is of the utmost importance to individuals and to society that attention should be watchfully bestowed upon children, both with respect to their health and their morals. Their future welfare in life depends upon this, and the important charge falls greatly upon the mother. Her first lesson—their talent being only imitation—should be that of obedience, mildly enforced; for, reason being the faculty of comparing ideas already presented to the mind, it cannot exist in a child, to whom few or no ideas have been presented.

With respect to the health of children, I fear the present management is not right. The mistaken indulgence of parents, in pampering and spoiling the appetites of children, lays the foundation of a permanent train of diseases, which an endless supply of medicines and nostrums will never restore to its pristine vigour. Skilful medical aid may, indeed, be of use, but nothing is so sure as a recurrence to a plain diet, temperance, and exercise. The next obstacle to remedy, I fear, will not be easily removed; for it is built upon the prejudices of mothers themselves, dictated by notions of fashion and gentility which have taken too deep a root. When folly has given the fashion, she is a persevering dame, and 'folly ever dotes upon her darling'.

161

Instead of impressing upon the minds of girls the importance of knowing household affairs, and other useful knowledge, and cultivating cheerfulness and affability along with the courtesies of life, they must undergo a training to befit them for appearing in frivolous company. To insure this, the mother, or some boarding school mistress, insists that these delicate young creatures be tightened up in a shape-destroying dress, and sit and move in graceful stiffness. They must not spring about or make use of their limbs, lest it might be called *romping*, and might give them so vulgar, so robust, and so red-cheeked a look that they would not appear *like ladies*. The consequence of this is, that they become like hot-house plants;—the air must not blow upon them;—and, in this state, they must attend routs and balls, and midnight assemblies, which send numbers of them to an untimely grave.* If they survive these trials, still they leave behind a want of health and vigour, which hangs upon them through life, and they become the nerveless outcasts of nature. They are then unfit to become the mothers of Englishmen; they twine out a life of *ennui*, and their generation dies out. I have all my life been grieved to find this description too often realized. It is paying too dear for female accomplishments. It is surely desirable that a change should take place, by which fashionable follies may be narrowed in their boundaries, and a better line drawn out; prescribed by propriety, affability, modesty, and good sense, on which the courtesies of life, and the invaluable embellishments of civilization, and everything graceful and charming in society, is founded. I wish the ladies of the British Isles may set the example, and take the lead in this, and be crowned with this brilliant diadem of civilization, studded with gems, so as to attract

* If these assemblies must be kept up—by the gentry who can afford it— they ought to be held in the day time, that those who attend them may get their natural rest at night.

the attention of the rest of the world, and illumine the paths which would lead them to pursue the same object and of banishing ignorant rudeness and vulgarity from the face of the earth.

If I could influence the fair sex, there is one thing to which I would draw their attention; and that is Horticulture; and, connected with this, I would recommend them, as far as convenient, to become Florists, as this delightful and healthy employment—which has been long enough in the rude hands of men—would entice them into the open air, stimulate them to exertion, and draw them away from their sedentary mode of life, mewed up in close rooms, where they are confined like nuns. This would contribute greatly to their amusement, and exhilarate their spirits. Every sensible man should encourage the fair sex to follow this pursuit. What would this world be without their help, to alleviate its burdens? It would appear a barren waste. It would no longer be a widespread garden of Eden, nor an earthly paradise within the reach of our enjoyments. May the fruits and flowers of it, reared and presented by their fair hands, ever operate as a charm in ensuring the attentions and unabating regard of all men! And of all good men it will. In thus dictating to them, no embarrassment can follow; and, if they ever know of the liberty I thus have taken, it will probably be when all embarrassments are, with me, at an end. And I can only further leave behind me a wish that health may eternally blush their cheeks, and virtue their minds.

Next in consideration to the ladies—whom they must in courtesy follow—are the freeholders of this favoured land. Such of these as, by their attainments, arrive at the degree of gentlemen, are, or ought to be, the pride and glory of every civilized country in the world. Placed in opulence and independence, with a liberal education, they are and must be looked up to as the patrons of every virtue in the people, who, in their station of life, may need such help to encourage them. May gentlemen never lose sight of this important duty, and ever be able to stem the torrent of gambling and dissipation; so that their ancient mansions may remain in their names for ever, as pledges of their worth, and as ornaments to the country. Without their countenance, arts and sciences, and artisans, would languish, industry would be paralysed, and barbarism again rear its benumbed hands and stupid head. It is to be hoped that the business of their wine vaults, their horses, and their dogs, may cease to be the main business of their lives, and only be looked to as matters of amusement wherewith to unbend their minds. And, as no man can, while he is in possession of his faculties, rest in happiness unless he is exercising them, and some hobby-horse must engage his attention, it therefore becomes a question for their consideration in what way they can best employ themselves. I would earnestly recommend that gentlemen should endeavour to improve their lands, and lay the foundation of fertilizing them: and instead of spending—perhaps squandering—their money in follies abroad, as far as possible, spend it at home. The late good and wise first Lord Ravensworth used to say, there was nothing grateful but the earth. 'You cannot,' said he, 'do too much for it; it will continue to pay tenfold the pains and labour bestowed upon it.' Estates so managed would then exhibit the appearance of clean-weeded nurseries. As an act of justice due to the industrious farmer, he ought, on entering upon his lease, to have his farm valued, and, when his lease is out, valued again; and whatever improvements he may have made, ought to be paid for on his leaving. I am well aware that these remarks may not be relished by those whose pride, dictated by the wish to domineer, will not give in to this fair proposal, for fear of the independent spirit it might rear; but it must be allowed that the landlord could come to no loss by it, and that the community would be greatly benefited by the adoption of such a plan. Those gentlemen who have moorlands, however exposed and bleak they may be, may yet do something to make them more productive, by enclosing them with dry stone dykes, beset and bound with ivy, and intersected with whin hedges;* and this shelter would form a bield for sheep and cattle, and besides would produce grass both in quantity and quality such as never grew there before.

The chief offices which gentlemen and freeholders are called upon to fulfil are, member of Parliament, magistrate, and juryman. The first is the most important; but, indeed, in that as well as the others, the requisite ingredients are honesty and intelligence. If we look at the wretched tools which boroughmongers obtrude upon the nation, we may anxiously look to the importance of electing gentlemen who will unceasingly and boldly oppose such men ever being allowed to sit as representatives. But these have already gone far on the road towards paralysing the British constitution, and establishing on its ruins an oligarchy, which is the worst and most odious of all governments, even scarcely excepting a mob government.

In the troublesome and gratuitous office of magistrate, great sagacity and penetration are requisite to enable the holders, in their political capacity, to discriminate between stretching too far the, perhaps, ill-defined, and often arbitrary laws, beyond the due bounds prescribed by justice and mercy. They ought to detest being made the tools of despotic acts of corruption, and being like Turkish Bashaws spread over the provinces. In their civil capacities, matters come more nearly home to them; and in this they have much need of cool deliberation, as well as extreme vigilance, for without these there would be no such thing

* The very clippings of which (as noticed before) would be healthful fodder for both sheep and cattle.

as living in peace while such numbers of the dregs of the people remain in ignorance and depravity. These latter do not know the meaning of either religion or morality, and it is only the strong arm of the law that can keep people of this description in order. Their evidence ought always to be suspected. Oaths have little weight: they are so used to them. One of our poets says—

> 'Of all the nauseous complicated crimes
> 'Which both infect and stigmatise the times,
> 'There's none which can with impious oaths compare,
> 'Where vice and folly have an equal share.'

But, bad as these reprobate oaths are, there are others which I think are still worse; and these are the numerous oaths used, and indeed imposed, on so many and on such improper occasions, where Omnipotence is impiously appealed to in all the little dirty transactions between man and man. It would be well to remember that 'an honest man's word is as good as his oath—and so is a rogue's too'. 'Tis a pity some better way cannot be hit upon to remedy these evils—perhaps a tattooing upon the shaved head might have some effect in checking swearing vices, especially in perjury, bearing false witness, and when a man is proved to have broken his word and his honour.

There is another vice, of an odious complexion, advancing with rapid strides to enormity, which cries aloud to be checked and that is the doubly degrading intercourse of illicit love and the effrontery with which base men become hardened and only laugh at their breaking down every barrier to modesty and virtue, and thus disrobing innocence, and rendering deformed that which ought to be the brightest feature of civilization. The crime to which I allude needs only to be examined to convince anyone of its cruelty to the fair sex, and its extensively demoralizing influence on society. Let any man ask himself how he would feel were his daughter or his sister to be betrayed or

166

to become a concubine of any man. This question ought to be fairly canvassed. Is it for the benefit of society or even of individuals that such a vice should be allowed? Although it will be allowed that men, devoid of honour and modesty, who have let loose their unbridled, bad passions, will not be easily stopped in their career yet, notwithstanding, this evil may be, by the strong arm of the law, greatly banished from the land, and innate modesty planted in its stead.

All men and women in health, and of good character, ought to be countenanced in marrying; and it is for them to consider whether they can properly rear and educate a family; and, should there be an over-abundant population, then colonization might be resorted to at the public expense; and this globe will be found large enough to hold additional millions upon millions of people. There are few contracts between human beings which should be more delicate than that of marriage. It is an engagement of the utmost importance to individuals and to society, and which of all others ought to be the most unbiassed; for it cannot be attended with honour, nor blessed with happiness, if it has not its origin in mutual affection. The rules to be observed in thus selecting and fixing the choice are few, simple, and easily understood. Both males and females, if of unsound constitution, ought to forbear matrimony. It is the duty of every man to endeavour to get a healthy woman for the sake of his children, and an amiable one for his own domestic comfort. The fair sex should observe the like rules. If a woman marries a man who has broken down his constitution by his own dissipation, or has imbibed a tainted one from his parents, she must not be surprised at becoming a nurse to him and his nerveless, puny, offspring. One cannot help wondering at the uncommon pains a gentleman will take in buying a horse, to see that the animal is perfectly sound, and without blemish, and that he should not take the same pains in choosing a wife, which is of infinitely more importance to him. He, perhaps to repair his shattered fortune, will marry any woman if she has plenty of money. She may, indeed, be the innocent heir to the full-charged hereditary diseases of a pair of voluptuous citizens, just as that may happen to be. No gentleman need to look far from his home, to be enabled to meet with an helpmate, possessing every requisite to make him happy; but, if he cannot meet with such a one, or cannot please himself in his own neighbourhood, he had better travel in search of one from Land's End to John o' Groat's House, than not get a proper partner as the mother of his children.

I have often thought that the children of gentlemen—boys particularly—are too soon put to school under improper restraints, and harassed with education before their minds are fit for it. Were they sent to the edge of some moor, to scamper about amongst whins and heather, under the care of some good old man—some mentor—who would teach them a little every day, without embarrassing them—they would there, in this kind of preparatory school, lay in a foundation of health, as well as education. If they were thus allowed to run wild by the sides of burns—to fish, to wade, and to splash in—they would soon find their minds intently employed in sports and pleasures of their own choosing. It would be found that youth so brought up, besides thus working out any little hereditary ailments, would never forget the charms of the country, which would impart to them a flow of spirits through life such as very few, or none, brought up in a town, ever know, and, besides this, lay in a strong frame-work on which to build a nervous constitution, befitting the habitation of an energetic mind and a great soul. Let anyone look at the contrast between men thus brought up, and the generality of early-matured Lilliputian plants, and he will soon see, with very few exceptions, the difference, both in body and mind, between them.

CHAPTER XVIII

The game laws — Riflemen — The fisheries — Grants in feudal times — A change necessary — The way to effect this — Remuneration to the present owners — Salmon formerly abundant in the Tyne — Spawning places — Weirs and dams — Impure water — Appointment of vigilant guards — Destruction of Salmon by the porpoise — Suggestions for catching the porpoise — Uses to which they may be applied — Necessity of protecting the parent fishes — Incredible number of the fry — The angler — Angling ought to be unchecked — Preserved waters debar the angler — Formation of Waltonian Societies recommended — Their duties — Constant beating of the streams to be discountenanced — Pought nets — Catching the fry in mill-races, and liming the burns, to be prohibited — Angling and its delights — Beautiful scenery — Permanent pools may be stocked with eels — Further reflections on the subject — Various friends.

THE game laws have for ages past been a miserable source of contention between those rendered unqualified by severe and even cruel game laws, and parties who had influence to get these laws enacted for their own exclusive privilege of killing the game. To convince the intelligent poor man that the fowls of the air were created only for the rich is impossible, and will for ever remain so. If it be pleaded that, because the game are fed on the lands of the latter, they have the exclusive right to them, this would appear to be carrying the notions of the sacredness of property too far; for even this ought to have its bounds; but were this conceded, as property is enjoyed by a rental, and as the farmers feed the game, they would appear to belong to them more properly than to any one else. I own I feel great repugnance in saying anything that might have a tendency to curtail the healthy enjoyments of the country gentleman, in his field sports, which his fortune and his

169

leisure enable him so appropriately to pursue; at the same time it is greatly to be regretted that anything—any over-stretched distinctions—should ever happen to make a breach between the poor and the rich. It is, however, to be wished that the unqualified man may find his attention engaged, and his mind excited in some other way (or by his business) than that of becoming a poacher. The strange propensity, however unaccountable, in almost all men TO KILL, and the pleasurable excitement to do so, is equally strong in the poacher as in the gentleman sportsman. This excitement, or an extreme desire to exhilarate the spirits, and to give them energy, as well as pleasure, pervades more or less, the minds of all mankind, and shows itself in every species of gambling, from cock-fighting, dog and man fighting, hunting, horse-racing, and even up to the acme of excitement—or excitement run mad—that of horrid war. I wish something more rational and better could be contrived to whet the mind and to rouse its energies; for certain it is that 'the heart that never tastes pleasure shuts up, grows stiff, and incapable of enjoyment'. The minds of men ought, therefore, to be unbent at certain times—especially in some constitutions—to prevent their becoming nerveless and hypochondriacal, the worst of all diseases, in which the mind sees everything with an obliquity of intellect, and creates numberless cruel and imaginary evils which continually surround and embarrass it. Only let a man who cannot employ himself with some hobby or other know that he is provided for, and has nothing to do, and it will soon be seen how *ennui*, with benumbing steps, will thrust itself upon him, and what a stupid and unhappy being he is.

If I have reasoned correctly in the foregoing observations, it is, then, desirable that sports and pastimes should be resorted to, that might, in many cases, turn out to public good. For this purpose, I have often thought that small sums might be subscribed and collected to be given as a prize to the best shot at a mark. The utility and national purpose of this scheme may at some time be felt; for, so long as surrounding despots can gather together immense mercenary armies, they ought to be effectually guarded against, and they certainly might be as effectually checked by hundreds of thousands of riflemen (including the militia), thus trained for the defence of the kingdom, at a comparatively small expense. They might have their bullets made of baked clay, which would probably be as efficient as those made of lead, and cost almost nothing.

The last subject I shall notice, as being kept up by unequal and unjust laws, is the fisheries, throughout the kingdom. The laws made respecting them originated in the times of feudal tyranny, when 'might was right', and everything was carried with a high hand. It was then easy for an overbearing aristocracy, by their influence, to get grants and charters made entirely on their own behalf. The rights of the community were set at nought, or were treated with contempt. But those days are passed away; the march of intellect is spreading over the world; and all public matters are now viewed with feelings of a very different kind than when such laws were made, and which ought to have been repealed long since; but they are still in force, and will continue so as long as the potent feelings of overstretched self-interest are allowed to guide those who have the power to keep the grasp of this their antiquated hold: for such can hear no reason against their private interest, however unanswerable it may be. No reasonable plea can ever be set up, to show that the fish of rivers ought to be the private property of any one. Can it be pretended that because a river or a rivulet, passes through an estate, whether the owner of it will or not, that the fish which breed in it, or which live in it, ought to be his? They are not like the game, which are all fed by the farmer, for fish

171

cost nobody anything; therefore, in common justice, they ought to belong to the public, and ought to be preserved for the public good, in every county through which the rivers pass, and be let at a rental from the clerk of the peace, and the money arising therefrom applied to making bridges and roads, or for county or other rates. Stewards ought to be appointed to receive the rents, and a committee of auditors elected annually, by ballot, as a check upon the management of the whole. If the fisheries were not thus rented, the public would derive little benefit from such an immense supply of food; for without they were thus disposed of, each county would soon be over-run with such numbers of poaching vagabonds as would become intolerable. All this, however, ought to be well considered; for, notwithstanding the selfish principle which dictated the original grants of the fisheries—long since obtained—the present possessors are not to blame, and suddenly to deprive any man of what he has been accustomed to receive may be deemed a harsh measure, and in some cases a cruel one; therefore some equitable sum should be paid to the owners at once, as a remuneration in lieu of all future claims; as fish ought not to be considered as an inheritance to descend to the heirs of any one.

From about the year 1760 to '67, when a boy, I was frequently sent by my parents to purchase a salmon from the fishers of the 'strike' at Eltringham ford. At that time, I never paid more, and often less, than three-halfpence per pound (mostly a heavy, guessed weight, about which they were not exact). Before, or perhaps about this time, there had always been an article inserted in every indenture in Newcastle, that the apprentice was not to be obliged to eat salmon above twice a week, and the like bargain was made upon hiring ordinary servants. It need not be added that the *salmo* tribe then teemed in abundance in the Tyne, and there can be little doubt that the same immense numbers would return to it again were proper measures pursued to facilitate their passage from the sea to breed. All animals, excepting fish, only increase, but they multiply, and that in so extraordinary a degree as to set all calculation at defiance. It is well known that they ascend every river, rivulet, and burn, in search of proper places to deposit their spawn; and this is the case both with those kinds which quit the sea, and those which never leave the fresh water. In their thus instinctively searching for proper spawning places, they make their way up to such shallows as one would think it impossible for any animal wanting legs and feet ever to crawl up to; therefore every improper weir or dam that obstructs their free passage ought to be thrown down, as they are one great cause of the salmon quitting the proper spawning places in the river, to return to spawn in the sea as well as they can; where, it is fair to conclude, their fry, or their roe, are swallowed up by other fish, as soon as they or it, are spread abroad along the shores.

It will readily be perceived, that the fishers' weirs are made chiefly with a view of preventing their neighbour fishers from coming in for their due share; but, were the fisheries let, as before named, the different fishing places would then be planned out by the stewards, as well as remedying other faults, with an impartial hand. There are, besides weirs and dams, other causes which occasion the falling off of the breed of salmon, by greatly preventing them from entering and making their way up rivers for the purpose of spawning. They have a great aversion to passing through impure water, and even snow-water stops them; for they will lie still, and wait until it runs off. The filth of manufactories is also very injurious, as well as the refuse which is washed off the uncleaned streets of large towns by heavy rains. Were this filth in all cases led away and laid on the land, it would be of great value to the

o   173

farmer, and persons should be appointed to do that duty, not in a slovenly or lazy manner, but with punctuality and despatch. In this the health and comfort of the inhabitants of towns ought to be considered as of great importance to them, as well as that of keeping the river as pure as possible on account of the fish.

Should the evils attendant upon weirs and dams, and other matters, be rectified, then the next necessary step to be taken should be the appointment of river conservators and vigilant guards to protect the kipper, or spawning fish, from being killed while they are in this sickly and imbecile state. They are then so easily caught, that, notwithstanding they are very unwholesome as food, very great numbers are taken in the night, which are eaten by poor people, who do not know how pernicious they are. But, should all these measures be found not fully to answer public expectation, the time now allowed for fishing might be shortened, and in some years, if ever found necessary, the fishing might be laid in for a season.

The next important question for consideration, is respecting what can be done to prevent the destruction of salmon on their first entering a river, and while they are in full perfection, by their most powerful and most conspicuously destructive enemy, the porpoise.

I have seen a shoal of porpoises, off Tynemouth, swimming abreast of each other, and thus occupying a space of apparently more than a hundred yards from the shore, seawards, and crossing the mouth of the river, so that no salmon could enter it. They went backward and forward for more than a mile, along shore, and with such surprising rapidity, that, in their course, they caused a foam to arise, like the breakers of the sea in a storm. Might not a couple of steam packets, with strong nets, sweep on shore hundreds of these at a time? Perhaps by giving premiums for catching them they might be greatly thinned, and their tough skins be tanned, or otherwise prepared, so as to be applied to some use. Oil might be obtained partly to pay for the trouble of taking this kind of fish; and, lastly, they might be used as an article of food. They were eaten formerly even by the gentry: and why not make the attempt to apply them to that purpose again? Perhaps, by pickling or drying them, and by other aids of cookery, they might prove good and wholesome; for every animal in season is so, which, when out of season, is quite the reverse.

If the parent fishes of the *salmo* tribe were protected, the fry would soon be seen to swarm in incredible numbers, and perhaps a pair of them would span more than all the anglers from the source of the mouth of any river could fairly catch in one season. Having from a boy been an angler, it is with feelings painfully rankling in my mind that I live in dread (from hints already given) of this recreation being abridged or stopped. Angling has from time immemorial been followed, and ought to be indulged in unchecked by arbitrary laws, as the birthright of everyone, but particularly of the sedentary and the studious. It is cruel to think of debarring the fair angler, by any checks whatever; the salmon fishers may, indeed, begrudge to see such fill his creel with a few scores of the fry; because what is taken might in a short time return to them as full-grown salmon (for all fish, as well as birds, return to the same places where they were bred); but, for reasons before-named, this selfishness should not be attended to for a moment, and the fisheries ought to be taken subject to this kind of toll or imaginary grievance.

I have always felt extremely disgusted at what is called preserved waters (except fish ponds); that is, where the fish in these waters are claimed exclusively as private property. The disposition which sets up claims of this kind is the same as would—if it could—sell the sea, and the use of the sun and the rain. Here the angler is debarred by the surly, selfish owner of the adjoining land, the pleasure of enjoying the most healthful and comparatively the most innocent of all diversions. It unbends the minds of the sedentary and the studious, whether it may be those employed at their desks, or 'the pale artist plying his sickly trade', and enables such to return to their avocations, or their studies, with renovated energy, to labour for their own or for the public good. But as anything, however good in itself, may be abused, therefore some regulations should be laid down as a guide to the fair angler in this his legitimate right, and some check imposed upon the poacher, who might be inclined to stop at nothing, however unfair. I think Waltonian societies would be all-sufficient to manage these matters, if composed of men of good character and good sense. There ought to be one of these societies established in the principal town in each district, and to have its honorary members branched out into the more distant parts. Perhaps a fine imposed, or even the frowns of the society, might be sufficient to deter poachers. The object ought to be, to regulate the times for angling, and to discountenance, or send to Coventry, such as spend almost the whole of their time in 'beating the streams'. They ought also to keep a watchful eye over such as care not how or in what manner they take fish, so as they may only get plenty of them. The 'Honourable Society of Waltonians' ought to use every means in their power to protect the 'glittering inhabitants of the waters' from being unfairly taken or destroyed. Pought nets ought to be prohibited, as well as all catching of the salmon fry in mill races, by putting thorn bushes into them, to stop their passing through, and then letting off the water. In this way, a cartload of these have often been known to be taken at once. Another method, still more destructive than this, is far too often put in practice; that is, what is called liming the burns. This ought to be utterly put a stop to by severe punishments. A clown, from ignorance—but, perhaps, from something worse—puts a few clots of unslaked, or quick, lime into a pool, or hole, in a burn, for the sake of killing a few trouts that he sees in it; and thus poisons the water running down to the rivulet, or the river, destroying every living creature to such a distance as may seem incredible. The attentive angler must sometimes have observed the almost invisible, incipient, living spawn in thousands, appearing only like floating mud, sunning themselves on a shallow sand-bank, which, as soon as the water thus poisoned reaches them, they drop down like mud indeed, and are no more seen.

How vividly do recollections of the enjoyment angling has afforded me return to the mind, now when those days have passed away, never more to return. Like the pleasing volume of the patriarch of anglers—Izaak Walton—volumes might yet be written to point out and to depicture the beautiful scenery of woods and water sides, in the midst of which the pleasures attendant upon this exhilarating and health-restoring, hungry, exercise is pursued. How many narratives of the exploits of the days thus spent might be raked up to dwell upon, when they are all over, like a pleasing dream!

Well do I remember mounting the stile which gave the first peep of the curling or rapid stream, over the intervening, dewy, daisy-covered holme—boundered by the early sloe, and the hawthorn-blossomed hedge—and hung in succession with festoons of the wild rose, the tangling woodbine, and the bramble, with their bewitching foliage—and the fairy ground—and the enchanting music of the lark, the blackbird, the throstle, and the blackcap, rendered soothing and plaintive by the cooings of the ringdove, which altogether charmed, but perhaps retarded, the march to the brink of the scene of action, with its willows, its alders, or its sallows—where early I commenced the day's patient campaign. The pleasing excitements of the angler still follow him, whether he is engaged in his pursuits amidst scenery such as I have attempted to describe, or on the heathery moor, or by burns guttered out by mountain torrents, and boundered by rocks or grey moss-covered stones, which form the rapids and the pools in which is concealed his beautiful yellow and spotted prey. Here, when tired and alone, I used to open my wallet and dine on fat meat and coarse rye bread, with an appetite that made me smile at the trouble people put themselves to in preparing the sumptuous feast; the only music in attendance was perhaps the murmuring burn, the whistling cry of the curlew, the solitary water ouzel, or the whirring wing of the moor game. I would, however, recommend to anglers not to go alone; a trio of them is better, and mutual assistance is often necessary.

It is foreign to my purpose to give any history, in this place, of the various kinds of fishes which anglers pursue; of this there is no need, for, I think, more treatises on this subject than on any other (except sermons) have been printed, to direct the angler to perfection in his art. But I cannot help noticing, as matter of regret, that more pains have not been taken to multiply fish, and to increase the breed of eels, as every permanent pool might so easily be fully stocked with them; and the latter are, when properly cooked, the most delicious of all fish kind. Walton has been particular in describing his mode of cooking them; but, unless he killed them beforehand, his method is a very cruel one, and is besides of not much consequence. After being killed, they then only need to be gutted and cooked unskinned in an unabating heat till they are done enough, for if they are cooked on a slow fire they are apt to turn oily and often disagree with some stomachs.

In thus dwelling on subjects which stimulate man eagerly to pursue the work of destruction, and to extend his power over those animals of which he considers himself as the lord and master, and that they are destined to contribute to his pleasures or to his support, yet he ought not totally to forget that what is sport to him is death to them, and that the less of cruelty the better.

I think, had I not begun so early to be an angler, and before feelings of tenderness had entered the mind, my eagerness for angling might have been, on this score, somewhat abated; but I argued myself into a belief that fish had little sense, and scarcely any feeling, and they certainly have very much less of either than any of the land animals; but we see through all nature that one kind of animal seems destined to prey upon another, and fishes are the most voracious of all.

Before concluding this memoir, it would be ungrateful in me not to acknowledge my obligations to my well-wishers, who have through life been steady in their friendships, and also in conferring their favours in the way of business. But a long list of names might seem tedious, and many of them are long ago numbered with the dead. For several years I had the favours of all the Banks in Newcastle, as well as those of most of the fitters, but a steady, underhand and dark influence detached several of both of these different employments from me. The first of friends to whom my thanks are due is the Corporation of Newcastle for their long and unabating favours as a body, and from time to time all its members individually. The most particular one of these was Alderman Archd. Reed. Among many of such friends, as I had reason to respect, both privately and publicly, one of the oldest in intimacy, affability and kindness was Anthony Easterley, Esq., of Coxlodge. Another whose eye of kindness watched my struggles to prosperity, was Mr Edmund Robson, patent saddler and hardware man, who, upon his suspecting that, in my publications, I might be labouring under difficulties, called me

179

one night out of Swarley's Club room, to say that he had two hundred pounds at my service whenever I pleased. This I considered as an uncommon thing in the world; but I startled at the idea of getting into any kind of debt, so I thanked him sincerely, and declined his kind offer. Two other friends of whom I had a high opinion for their truth and integrity were William Leadbitter, saddler and hardware man, and Francis Coates, bookseller. The former died 3rd August 1801, aged 38, and the latter on 24th February 1803. An intimacy of long standing had subsisted between the Crawhall family and mine, and I had a particular regard for two of the brothers, Thomas and Joseph, the latter was particularly an amateur of the arts and excelled as a painter, for which nature had furnished him with the requisite powers, but in this he was taken off by his business of a rope maker. I might name others of the like character, but they have left this world long ago, a few of such only being left, both as friends and social companions, and thus noticing them puts me in mind of its being like creeping out of this world, or at least out of this kind of society, for excepting that of my own happy fireside, I think I shall bid all adieu. My warm friend, Mr William Maving, brush manufacturer, his brother Robert, builder, Mr Alexander Reid, china dealer, Mr Adam Hutton, hardwareman, Mr William Wilson, solicitor, Mr Robert Gruisburn, stationer (and occasionally some others) were the last with whom I spent my social evenings. The full moon was generally the signal for our assembling, when we gave full vent to what was uppermost in our minds. At other times some of my evenings were spent much in the same way in company with John Marshall, printer, and others, along with John Ambrose Williams, the editor of the *Durham Chronicle*. It might be tedious to swell out a list of names or dwell upon the occasional visits of men of sense and ability who from time to time spent their evenings with me. Mr Anthony Scott, of Southwick Pottery, was one of these, and when he was in Newcastle he seldom missed this kind of social communication of our sentiments. On these occasions my ingenious self-taught friend, Mr Robert Wilson, engineer and engine maker, always made one of our party. In their company the longest evening seemed very short. I was also often visited by poor old Mr John Rastrick, of Morpeth, who, in his day, was, by many men of judgment, accounted one of the most able and ingenious engineers in the kingdom. He died June 1826, aged 88. I also spent much time (while he remained in Newcastle) with my gallant friend Colonel Wemyss, of Wemyss Hall in Fifeshire, formerly of the 11th Regiment of Foot, and afterwards Colonel of the Fifeshire militia. He was ardent in his pursuit after mechanical knowledge, and greatly valued ingenious workmen in that way, and begged I would introduce him to such—he said 'he cared not what kind of coat they wore'—and I was not long in introducing him to those, in whose company he gained the information he wanted, and seemed highly gratified.

CHAPTER XIX

Not having seen Edinburgh since August 1776, I longed to see it again, and accompanied with my Jane and Isabella, we set out on this journey on the 11th August 1823, and went through by coach on that day. I always thought highly of Edinburgh and its bold and commanding situation; but the new town, or city of palaces, as it is now sometimes called, had been added to it since I had seen it. But all these splendid buildings are of trivial import compared with the mass of intellect and science which had taken root and had been nurtured and grown up to such a height as to rival, and perhaps to outstrip, every other city in the world. Our stay in it was only a fortnight; and this was a busy time with us, both as to its being taken up with the kindness and hospitality we met with everywhere, as well as in visiting its various scientific and other establishments. It being at a vacation season, when most of the learned professors were out of town, we saw only Professors Jameson and Wallace, and the kindness of these gentlemen I never can forget. We were often at the table of the former surrounded by men of learning and science who visited him, on which occasions the amiable manners and affability of his sisters, the Misses Jameson, made every place appear like a home. The civility of Professor Wallace was also of the most friendly complexion. He showed me the use of

182

the Eidograph, an instrument which he invented for the purpose of either reducing or enlarging any drawing or design most accurately to any size that might be required. We also visited Patrick Neil, Esq., along with the Misses Jameson, and were much pleased with seeing the tamed birds and other curiosities which embellished his little paradise. His uncommon kindness will ever remain impressed upon our memories. We also often called upon my friend, Mr Archibald Constable, accounted the first bookseller in Scotland; and, although he was unwell at the time, partook of his kind attentions. Mr Robert Miller, bookseller, also did everything in his power which affability and kindness could dictate to make us altogether pleased with Edinburgh. Our friend, Mr William Reid, bookseller, Leith, did the same, only with this difference, that his attentions were unceasing, and Mrs Reid's and his hospitality made their house a kind of home to us. Almost constantly accompanied by Mr Reid as our guide, we visited every place, and he besides introduced us to such artists as I did not know. In this way he took us to Mr William Allan, the historical painter, to the rooms of the splendid exhibition of the paintings of the late Sir Henry Raeburn, Bart., to Mr Stewart, the engraver, to Mr [James] Howe, the portrait and animal painter, and to the painting room of others, who were absent. To some other artists who were known to me I spent some time in several calls. These consisted of my old friend Mr Nasmyth, the excellent landscape painter; my townsmen, Mr William Nicholson, and Mr Ewbank, both of whom were eminent painters; and Mr Thomas Coulson, distinguished in his line as an ornamental and house painter. I also made several calls upon Mr James Kirkwood, now up in years, and past his work, but who had in his prime led the way to excellence, particularly in writing engraving, in which he was succeeded by his son and grandson. I also paid my respects to the son and successor of my kind friend of former days, the late Mr Hector Gavin, and the same to the sons and successors of the late Mr D. Lizars. All these, in my estimation, were doing credit to their instruction as engravers, and all these artists, as well as the painters, had attained in their various ways to that degree of excellence which did honour to Edinburgh, now the seat of learning, and rendered brilliant by the gems both of art and science with which it is adorned. We left Edinburgh on the 23rd August 1823, and I think I shall see Scotland no more. I think so well of these, our northern countrymen, that in most things they may serve as a pattern of both good sense and good conduct worthy of imitation by the other less civilized nations of the world. I have almost forgotten to name my being introduced to Messrs Ballantyne and Robertson, lithographic printers. Whilst I was in their office, the latter pressed me to make a sketch on the stone for him. I was then preparing to leave Edinburgh, and the only time left me was so short that I was obliged to draw this sketch before breakfast the next morning, and the proofs were taken from it on the same day. In doing this, though very slight, I could see what that manner of making prints was capable of.

After my journeys (long ago) to Cherryburn were ended, I used, as formerly, seldom to miss going in the mornings to Elswick Lane, to drink whey, or buttermilk, and commonly fell in with a party who went there for the same purpose; and this kind of social intercourse continued for many years. I also, at that time, on the Sunday afternoons, went to visit and contemplate in the church-yards, and there give vent to my mind, in feelings of regret, and in repeating a kind of soliloquy over the graves of those with whom I had been intimate, but as this at length appeared to be unavailing sorrow, I left it off.

'And then I lov'd to haunt lone burial places,
    Pacing the church-yard path with noiseless tread,
To pore on new-made graves for ghastly traces,—
    Brown crumbling bones of the forgotten dead.'

I recounted in my memory the numbers of my friends thus put by to be forgotten, amongst the millions of others who had been for longer or shorter periods also in this world, and who have passed away into oblivion. Some men from the first, as soon as they die, are quite unnoticed— some are remembered only for a day and some a little while longer, and even the 'frail memorial'—erected to *'perpetuate the memory'* of those who had been esteemed— seemed to be of little avail, and their mementoes, as well as those decked out with ornamented flatteries, would, in time, all go to decay, and be no longer remembered than until all who once knew them were also dead; and the numbers of both the one and the other appeared to me to be so immense that to estimate them seemed impossible, and like attempting to count the grains of sand on the seabeach. It is thus that the grave swallows all up without distinction. The true estimate of their various merits can only be known to the Creator of all. It appears clear to those whose souls habitually adore and commune with Him, while they remain in this state of probation, that He will, in His infinite goodness, wisdom, truth, justice, and mercy—place everyone, on quitting this mortal abode, in the unknowable worlds befitting their reception.

Besides the temporary mementoes dedicated to private worth, others of a different character may have their use. Monuments might therefore be erected to those who have, by their virtues and patriotism, promoted the happiness of mankind. It is a debt of gratitude due to the Author of our being for the loan of departed worth, and may stimulate others 'to do so likewise'. The posthumous praise or blame of the world is to them of no avail; they are done

185

with all things on this side of Time, and are out of the reach of both the one and the other.

While I was pursuing my wild ramblings in the Highlands, and beheld with admiration the great projecting rocks so often to be seen holding up their bare heads to the winds, it struck me that it was a great pity they could not be converted to some use: and the best I could think of was, that the illustrious names of Wallace and Bruce—as well as those of their other worthies—should be inscribed upon them, to hold up their heads with these names to the sun for ever. I have often thought since, that the bare rocks in other parts of our islands might with good effect be filled up in the same way. The first name to be fixed upon ought to be that of Alfred the Great, followed by many others—statesmen, patriots, philosophers, poets, etc.— who have shone out like polished diamonds, and who have embellished and illumined this country, and civilized the world. Their venerated names, with their maxims, or quotations from their works, would fill up many of these rocks, which are waiting for them, and might make all who beheld them inclined to profit by, or to imitate, their virtues. How many incomparably good, wise, and beautiful texts from the Bible might also with great propriety be added to fill up every vacant spot. I often lamented that I had not the means to enable me to be at the expense of getting such quotations inscribed in this way. Often, while angling on a hot, sunny day, which slackened my sport, I have sat down by the water side, and thought over some of the beautiful lines of our poets, fit to be applied in this way; and remember my having thought of those lines of Cunningham, which I would, if I could have afforded it, have committed to the care of a rock. He says:

'How smooth that rapid river glides
Progressive to the deep!
The poppies pendent o'er its sides
Have lull'd the waves to sleep.

> 'Pleasure's intoxicated sons!
>   Ye indolent! ye gay!
> Reflect,—for as the river runs
>   Time wings his trackless way.'

How easy would it be for gentlemen to get the names of the illustrious dead thus inscribed upon rocks; or, where that could not be done, to erect pillars, or small obelisks, over copious springs (like the holy wells of old), to contain such inscriptions as those I have hinted at, and thus leave these their marks behind them; and which would long continue to put the passing stranger in mind of some religious, moral, or patriotic sentiment; and, while he was refreshing himself by quenching his thirst, he might be put in mind that—

> 'Man wants but little here below,
> Nor wants that little long.'

CHAPTER XX

HAVING already noticed my beginnings, or first efforts, in engraving on wood, and as at that time this department of the arts was at the very lowest ebb in this country, and, I believe, also in every other country in Europe, it may perhaps be of some use, or at least may excite some curiosity, to know the part I took in renewing, or bringing into use, this to me new art, as far as I was able, with the slender means in my hands, and the many difficulties I had to contend with and surmount, before anything like an approach towards perfection could be arrived at. I ought first distinctly to state that, at that time, it never entered into my head that it was a branch of art that would stand pre-eminent for utility, or that it could ever in the least compete with engraving on copper. I ought also to observe that no vain notions of my arriving at any eminence ever passed through my mind, and that the sole stimulant with me was the pleasure I derived from imitating natural objects (and I had no other patterns to go by), and the opportunity it afforded me of making and drawing my designs on the wood, as the only way I had in my power of giving vent to a strong propensity to gratify my feelings in this way. In process of time, however, as I began to

188

improve, and seeing the practical use printers were making of wood-cuts, the utility and importance of them began to be unfolded to my view; and the more I have since thought upon the subject, the more I am confirmed in the opinions I have entertained, that the use of wood-cuts will know no end, or, so long as the importance of printing is duly appreciated and the liberty of the press held sacred.

The first difficulty I felt, as I proceeded, was in getting the cuts I had executed printed so as to look anything like my drawings on the blocks of wood, or corresponding to the labour I had bestowed upon the cutting of the designs. At that time pressmen were utterly ignorant as to any proper effect that was to be produced; or even, if one of them possessed any notions of excellence beyond the common run of workmen, his materials for working were so defective that he could not execute even what he himself wished to accomplish. The common pelt balls then in use, so daubed the cut, and blurred and overlapped its edges, that the impression looked disgusting. To remedy this defect, I was obliged carefully to shave down the edges round about; and this answered the end I had in view. The next difficulty was worse to surmount, and required a long time to get over it; and that was, to lower down the surface on all the parts I wished to appear pale, so as to give the appearance of the required distance; and this process will always continue to call forth and to exercise the judgment of every wood engraver, even after he knows what effect his *careful pressman* may be enabled to produce, from this his manner of cutting. On this all artists must form their own ideas. I think no exact description can be laid down as a rule for others to go by; they will by practice have to find out this themselves. While I was patiently labouring and contending with difficulties which I could not overcome, I was shown some impressions from wood-cuts done long ago, with cross-hatching, such as I thought

P   189

I should never be able to execute. These were wood-cuts by Albert Durer, and perhaps some others of his day, in the collection of the Rev John Brand, the Newcastle Historian; and from these I concluded that Albert Durer must have had some very easy way of loading his blocks with such an useless profusion of cross-hatching, or he would not have done them so, unless, indeed, he had found out some easy means of etching the wood (or perhaps metal plates), quite unknown to me; but, if otherwise,I then, in changing my opinion, could think of no other way than that he must have cut his blocks on the plank or side way of the wood, on which it would be more easy to pick out the interstices between the squares, or the lozenge-shaped lines, than as I (at that time) thought it possible to do on the end way of the wood. One of these plank blocks, said to have been drawn by Albert Durer, was shown to me by my kind friend George Allan, Esq., of the Grange, Darlington. The drawing, which was done with great accuracy, seemed to me to have been done by a crow-quill, with a kind of varnish ink, the strokes of which, from their regularity, looked as if they had been printed from a well-executed copper plate, and transferred to the block. After labouring for some time, endeavouring to produce the like effect on my blocks, on the end way of the wood, not indeed to my satisfaction, I felt mortified in not succeeding to my wish; and I then began to think the impressions must have been printed from two blocks. This, indeed, I soon found to be quite easy to do, as well as being beautifully correct; and any artist may see this in a few minutes, by cutting parallel lines on a piece of wood, and from it taking, by his hand, an impression on a piece of paper, and then again inking the same cut, and printing it in the same way, either directly in a cross or in an oblique direction, upon the first impression. This can also easily be done, from two cuts, at a printing press, and is much easier to do, and better than the labour necessarily bestowed upon one cross-hatched block. When I had accomplished this, and satisfied myself that the process was both simple and perfect, as to obtaining the object I so much wanted, my curiosity on this score ceased, and I then concluded that in this way the cross-hatching might be set aside as a thing of no use at all. The artists indeed of the present day have brought it to such a pitch of perfection that I do not know that it can be carried any further; and in this they have also been so marvellously aided by the improved methods now used in printing their cuts, that one would be led to conclude that this department has also attained to perfection; and, had this not been the case, the masterly execution of wood-cuts, either by crossed lines, or otherwise, would have continued to be beheld with disgust or contempt. I have long been of opinion that the cross-hatching of wood-cuts, for book work, is a waste of time; as every desired effect can be much easier obtained by plain parallel lines. The other way is not the legitimate object of wood engraving. Instead of imitating the manner of copper etchings, at a great cost of labour and time, on the wood, such drawings might have been as soon etched on the copper at once; and, where a large impression of any publication was not required, the copper plate would have cost less, and lasted long enough for the purpose intended. I never could discover any additional beauty or colour that the crossed strokes gave to the impression, beyond the effect produced by plain parallel lines. This is very apparent when to a certainty the plain surface of the wood will print as black as ink and balls can make it, without any further labour at all; and it may easily be seen that the thinnest strokes cut upon the plain surface will throw *some light* on the subject or design: and, if these strokes are made wider and deeper, it will receive more light; and if these strokes, again, are made still wider, or of equal thickness to the black lines, the colour these pro-

191

duce will be a grey; and the more the white strokes are thickened, the nearer will they, in their varied shadings, approach to white, and, if quite taken away, then a perfect white is obtained. The methods I have pursued appear to me to be the simple and easy perfection of wood engraving for book printing, and, no doubt, will appear better or worse according to the ability of the artist who executes them. The first time I ever heard anything about colour being produced by plain engraving was in the compliments paid me by Dr Thomas Stout, for my engraving on his large silver box. The device, or design, I have now forgotten, but never what he said on the occasion; and from that time I attempted *colour* upon the wood; and, though I felt much difficulty in my attempts at producing it, yet the principle is there, and will shine out under the skill and management of any eminent engraver on wood who is gifted with a painter's eye; and his work will be complete if seconded by a pressman of ability, who may happen to have a talent and fellow-feeling for the art.

I have before noticed my lowering down the surface of the wood, in order to produce the effect of distance, and the same thing holds good with every figure where different shades of colour are desired. Leaving the surface of the block without being pared down at all, and relying only on the lines being left thicker or smaller for producing the requisite depth of shade, this surface thus left acts as a support to the more delicate lines, which have been engraved on the lowered part of the cut. After all the parts are thus lowered, a further paring down of the edges of the various figures which the cut contains may be necessary to prevent their appearing as if surrounded by a white line. The delicate lines thus lowered, so as to print pale or distant parts, and thus protected by the stronger lines left on the surface —a wood cut, with care, will print an incredible number: how many it may be difficult exactly to say; but it once happened that I had the opportunity given me of guessing pretty nearly at this, from the calculation of the late Mr S. Hodgson, when he called upon me with a gentleman (a stranger to me), who seemed extremely curious to know everything respecting engraving on wood. One of his queries was made with a view of ascertaining how many impressions a wood cut would print. Not having anything in mind at the moment, to enable me to satisfy him, I began to consider, and it then struck me that a little delicate cut —a view of Newcastle—was done for Mr H. many years before, as a *fac* for his newspaper. I then turned to the date in my ledger, when he calculated exactly, and found it had printed above 900,000. This cut was continued in the newspaper several years afterwards. It was protected in the manner before noticed by a strong black line, or border, surrounding it, within which the surface was lowered previous to cutting the view. This cut is still kept; and, except being somewhat damaged by being tossed about amongst other castaway cuts, might, by being a little repaired, yet print many thousands. This is mentioned with a view to show the great length of time that cuts done in this way will last, if they are carefully adjusted to the height of the type, and kept out of the hands of ignorant, rude pressmen.

I am of opinion that cuts done in the manner called surface-cutting cannot stand anything like so large an impression as when they are lowered thus; for the delicate lines, when left on the surface, must soon break down from the heavy pressure to which they are exposed.

CHAPTER XXI

IT is foreign to my present purpose to criticize the works of brother artists of the present day. I behold their excellent productions with pleasure; in them there is no falling off: they surpass those of the artists of the olden times. I cannot, however, help lamenting that, in all the vicissitudes which the art of wood engraving has undergone, some species of it is lost and done away: I mean the large blocks with the prints from them, so common to be seen when I was a boy in every cottage and farm house throughout the country. These blocks, I suppose, from their size, must have been cut on the plank way on beech, or some other kind of close-grained wood; and from the immense number of impressions from them, so cheaply and extensively spread over the whole country, must have given employment to a great number of artists, in this inferior department of wood cutting; and must also have formed to them an important article of traffic. These prints, which were sold at a very low price, were commonly illustrative of some memorable exploits, or were, perhaps, the portraits

194

of eminent men, who had distinguished themselves in the service of their country, or in their patriotic exertions to serve mankind. Besides these, there were a great variety of other designs, often with songs added to them of a moral, a patriotic, or a rural tendency, which served to enliven the circle in which they were admired. To enumerate the great variety of these *pictures* would be a task. A constant one in every house, was 'King Charles' Twelve Good Rules'. Amongst others were representations of remarkable victories at sea, and battles on land, often accompanied with portraits of those who commanded, and others who had borne a conspicuous part in these contests with the enemy. The house at Ovingham, where our dinner poke was taken care of when at school, was hung round with views or representations of the battles of Zorndorff,* and several others; also the portraits of Tom Brown, the valiant grenadier, of Admiral Haddock, Admiral Benbow, and other portraits of admirals. There was also a representation of the *Victory* man-of-war, of 100 guns, commanded by Admiral Sir John Balchen, and fully manned with 1,100 picked seamen and volunteers, all of whom, with this uncommonly fine ship, were lost—sunk to the bottom of the sea. This was accompanied by a poetical lament of the catastrophe, part of which was—

'Ah! hapless Victory, what avails
Thy towering masts, thy spreading sails.'

Some of the portraits, I recollect, now and then to be met with, were very well done in this way, on wood. In Mr Gregson's kitchen, one of this character hung against the wall many years. It was a remarkably good likeness of Captain Coram. In cottages everywhere were to be seen the 'Sailor's Farewell' and his 'Happy Return', 'Youthful Sports', and the 'Feats of Manhood', 'The Bold Archers Shooting at a Mark', 'The Four Seasons', etc. Some sub-

* [Defeat of a Russian army by Frederick the Great in 1758.]

jects were of a funny—others of a grave character. I think the last portraits I remember were of some of the rebel lords and 'Duke Willy'. These kind of wood-cut pictures are long since quite gone out of fashion, which I feel very sorry for, and most heartily wish they could be revived. It is desirable, indeed, that the subjects should be well chosen; for it must be of great importance that such should be the case; as, whatever can serve to instil morality and patriotism into the minds of the whole people must tend greatly to promote their own happiness and the good of the community. All men, however poor they may be, ought to feel that this is their country, as well as it is that of the first nobleman of the land; and, if so, they will be equally as interested in its happiness and prosperity.

There is another way, not yet indeed entered upon, of similar import to the foregoing, in which prints might with good effect be made of subjects fit to embellish almost every house throughout our country: and that is from wood blocks printed in colours, like paper-hangings. Having seen some such done by paper-stainers, so as almost to equal good paintings, leads me to wish that this method could be pursued—for the same ends as those already noticed. The most remarkable productions of art of this kind from blocks done to print in colour, like beautiful little paintings, were sent to me by Gubitz, of Berlin; they might indeed be said to be perfection. Several impressions from duplicate or triplicate blocks, printed in this way, of a very large size, were also given to me, as well as a drawing of the press from which they were printed, many years ago, by an old man of the name of Jackson (Jean Baptiste Jackson), who had been patronized by the King of France; but, whether these prints had been done with the design of embellishing the walls of houses in that country, I know not. They had been taken from paintings of eminent old masters, and were mostly Scripture pieces. They were

196

well drawn, and perhaps correctly copied from the originals, yet in my opinion none of them looked well. Jackson left Newcastle quite enfeebled with age, and, it was said, ended his days in an asylum, under the protecting care of Sir Gilbert Elliot, Bart., at some place on the Border near the Teviot, or on Tweedside.

Whether the speculations here noticed may be thought worthy of being acted upon, I know not, but it is not to any of the above noticed ways of wood-cutting that my attention is directed: it is, in my ardent desire to see the *stroke* engraving on wood carried to the utmost perfection, that I hope the world will be gratified; and I trust the time is not distant when its superior excellence will be seen, particularly in landscape scenery, so as to surpass copper-plate engravings. The effect to be produced by wood engraving has not, in that way, yet been tried, nor its powers made apparent. This is, I think, to be attained by two, or even more, blocks being employed, on one print, so that a greater and more natural effect—as to colour and softness—may be produced. I am well aware that some difficulty may arise, as to bringing off a clear impression of fine strokes from so large a surface, but in this age of mechanical improvement and invention, I think this apparent difficulty will readily be got over. Perhaps printing from a roller, instead of an even down pull, may easily accomplish this business. I have often thought, had William Woollett been a wood engraver, he would have shown its excellence long ago: his prints from copper have not been equalled; but, from the nature of the wood, and the effect it produces, he would have advanced a step further, and on it have outdone his excellence on copper. If I live, health and sight continued, I will make the attempt to show that all this is not a visionary theory. Should I not live to get this Memoir printed under my own inspection for the benefit of yourself, your brother and sisters—or whether it will ever be printed at all, I know not—but at any rate the manuscript itself which I leave to my dear Jane will satisfy her, were that necessary, how ardently I have ever wished well to arts and artists; and though, in my endeavours to show this, I have often been thwarted and disappointed, yet I never lost sight of my object, nor became disheartened in my struggles to fight through, and surmount numberless difficulties and bars thrown in my way.

You know a part of those I met with in the course of my business, in which my time was misspent, and also the waste of it bestowed upon useless and wicked pupils. I know you wish me to give you a history and description of such; but to do so would be an irksome task and I cannot now be troubled to think about it. I shall however give you a curtailed list (as a whole), and only speak of such as served out their time. I have already noticed my brother John as my first pupil, and therefore have little further to say respecting him, only adding that nature seemed to have befitted him for becoming a first-rate wood-engraver, but, at the time he was with me, the thoughts of aiming at excellence, did not enter into our heads, and he left this world at the time when it was only begun to be looked upon as a matter of any interest. Our first apprentice was John Laws, who was brought up as a silver engraver, and I think he never touched upon the wood. His turn was directed to the ornamental, and chiefly in the branch of what is called bright engraving, and at this kind of work he excelled, and is perhaps the best at this day. With it he also follows the business of a farmer, at Heddon Laws, the place of his nativity. We greatly respected him for his honesty, sobriety, civil deportment and attention. The next for whom we had a great regard, for the like reasons, was John Johnson, whom we put to do engraving on wood as well as other kinds of work. I think he would have shone out in the former branch, but he died of a fever, at about the age of 22 when only beginning to give great promise of his future excellence. Our next apprentice was Robert Johnson,* who did not incline to do wood-cutting, and, preferring copper-plate engraving, he was almost wholly employed in that way, and in it attained to great excellence. Besides that, he became great as a draughtsman and colourist; but as he was of so delicate a constitution that he could not bear confinement, we, for that reason, set him to work to make sketches and views, where he had both air and exercise. It may be necessary to give a more detailed history than ordinary of this boy, on account of the unceasing pains I bestowed upon his tuition, and my reasons for doing so. His mother had been long a servant in father's house, where she became a great favourite, and like one of our family. When she married, this boy Robert was her first-born; and when he was christened I was to have been his godfather. This however did not happen, for while I was, for that purpose, on my road near to Ovingham, where the ceremony was to be performed, being only about 16 or 17 years old and exceedingly bashful, I could not think of appearing before a congregation of people, and when, on getting to the top of the 'pantin brae', the bells began to ring for church, I felt so abashed at the thought of what I had to do that I 'turned tail'—went a little back, and crossed the river upon the top of the Fishermen's Weir by stepping from one stob to another, which are driven in to support the wicker work and stones of which the weir is formed. I then went to Cherryburn, and after getting some refreshment, returned again to Newcastle. In the meantime my father and mother stood sponsors for the child. As the boy grew up, he having been almost constantly told he was to be my apprentice, he looked up to me as a kind of deity, and having been, at

* [1770–1796, a cousin of John Johnson.]

every opportunity, kept closely employed in drawing and making pictures, which were regularly shewn my father and mother and through them to myself, he thus came very early into practice. As soon as he attained somewhere about his thirteenth year friends began to act upon the scheme so long projected, of putting these intentions in force, and in this business my father and mother stood foremost as the warm friends of the boy, and begged I would always shew the same disposition towards him, and to take him under my fostering care. He was about a year too young to be bound as an apprentice; but I took him into the house till the proper time arrived, when he was bound to my partner and myself for seven years. He was mostly employed at drawing, and was also at intervals practising himself in the use of the graver, and in etching on copper; but being very delicate in his health we were careful not to confine himself too closely at anything. It may perhaps be useful to artists to know how I thought it best to order and manage such a tender and pampered boy. The system I began upon was that of rigid temperance— he got no medicine from me. My sister Ann, at that time kept my house, and to get her to second me in my plans I experienced great difficulty, chiefly from her fears 'that folks would raise a report that we hungered him'; but I resolutely persisted in my plan, and would not allow her to put in her word against it. I began by cutting off for him almost everything he had given to him to eat. The animal food with which I helped his plate at dinner, did not exceed in bulk the size of three of my fingers, to this was added a portion of vegetables. For breakfast and supper he got a pint of milk with leavened rye bread, to which last article I did not prevent him from helping himself. He had not been kept to this kind of temperate or pinched regimen above two months, till such an alteration for the better took place in his looks as seemed surprising, so much so

200

that his mother, when she called to see him held up her hands in astonishment at seeing this change from a pale, pasty, sickly look to that of his having cheeks blushed with health like a rose, and this same plan was pursued while he remained under my roof.* The methods I took to learn him his business was also of a piece with his mode of living. I did not keep him so long at work as to tire him, with whatever job he might be put to do, especially in drawing, but then whatever I gave him to copy was to be done perfectly correct, and he dreaded to show me work that was not so, although I never scolded him, but only, if I was not pleased, I put the drawing away from me without saying a word. Sometimes I remember saying O fie! and in this way of treatment he attained to great accuracy. The next thing I put him to was that of colouring, chiefly my own designs, and these occasioned me much time and labour, for I made it a point of drawing these with great accuracy, and with a very delicately pencilled outline. The practical knowledge I had attained in colouring was imparted to him, and he saved me a great deal of what I considered a loss of my time in being taken up in this way, and besides he soon coloured them in a style superior to my hasty productions of that kind. Indeed, in this way he became super excellent; and, as I conceived, he could hardly be equalled in his water colour drawing of views and landscapes by any artist. For some time I continued to sketch in his figures, but at length he needed none of my help in this way. I remember of his once coming to me, and begging I would draw or sketch in a tree for him. 'No, Robert,' said I, 'but I will direct you to a place where you will see such a tree as you never saw painted by any artist in your life,' and that was a tree then growing in Adonis's Grove. He

---

* Another of my plans was to make growing boys exercise with dumb-bells half an hour or so before bed time. I believe were this practised by the sedentary of both sexes, it would go a great way to banish consumption.

201

went and endeavoured to do justice to his pattern, and I do not know that anyone could have made a better likeness. As soon as the time arrived that he became entitled to have wages from us, this tempted his father and mother to leave the country and to reside in Newcastle, and to have him to board with them. How he was managed as to his diet with them I know not, but it soon appeared to have been a wrong treatment in this respect, for he soon lost his health and was from that time seldom out of the hands of the doctor, and at one period of his apprenticeship he was about a year absent from our employment either in the country or in being nursed with watchful care at home. He however became quite well by the time he was freed from his servitude with us, and he then commenced painting and engraving on his own account. In the former art he seemed to be much patronized, and had, I believe, turned his attention to oil-painting. The last of his efforts in this line was done under the patronage of the Earl of Buchan* by whom he was employed to copy some portraits and perhaps some other things at [Kenmore], where he took ill of a fever and died in the year 1796 and in the 26th of his age. It always appeared that he would have become great as a painter; but a delicate constitution and want of stamina prevented this. I have often thought it was a great mistake in parents, and a very common one, to fix upon some sedentary employment for their tender delicate boy, when, perhaps, had he been sent to sea, or some other out-door work, where he would be exposed to fresh air and exercise, he might have become a healthy stout and hale man. My friends having often expressed a wish that I would give some account of my pupils has occasioned me to dwell thus long upon that of Robert Johnson; but I think it unnecessary to notice others who were not gifted with talents, and some others again who had neither one good

* [Bewick is mistaken here. It was the Earl of Breadalbane.]

property nor another, and with whom I had much vexation and reason to complain. The first of my pupils who made a figure in London, after my brother, as a wood-engraver, was Charlton Nesbit.* He went at a nick of time when wood-cuts seemed to claim something like universal attention, and, fortunately for that art, it was under the guidance of the ingenious John Thurston, who pencilled his designs, stroke by stroke on the wood, with the utmost accuracy, and it would appear that Nesbit was the first, by his mechanical excellence, to do justice to these designs. Henry Hole and John Anderson preceded Nesbit. The next of my pupils, who chiefly turned his attention to wood-engraving, was Edward Willis, who, while he remained with me, was much upon a par with Nesbit, but did not equal him in the mechanical excellence Nesbit had attained to in London. I had a great regard for Edward Willis, on account of his regular good behaviour while he was under my tuition. He has now been long a resident in London. My nephew, John Harrison, was chiefly employed on writing engraving; he died of epileptic fits, and was buried at North Shields between two trees near the foot-path. Henry White, from London, was engaged to me to serve out the remainder of his apprenticeship, when his master, the late Mr Lee, died. When the term of his engagement with me was ended, he returned to London, and chiefly turned his attention to the imitation of sketchy cross-hatching on wood, from the inimitable pencil of Mr Cruikshank, and, perhaps, some other artists in this same way. Henry White, appears to have taken the lead of others who followed that manner of cutting, which shortly became *quite the Ton*. Another of my pupils of distinguished ability, both as a draftsman and wood-engraver, was Luke Clennell,† whose melancholy history will be well

* [1775–1838.]
† [1781–1840. Insane from 1817 until his death.]

remembered by the artists of London and elsewhere, and the sympathetic feelings which were drawn forth and shown to him by a generous public by their subscriptions to a print of the battle of Waterloo from his painting of the decisive charge of the Guards on that eventful day. The next of my pupils was Isaac Nicholson, who was both a good apprentice and a good artist. His engravings on wood are clearly or honestly cut, as well as accurately done from his patterns. He did not pursue his business in London, but carries it on in Newcastle. The next of my pupils, and one of the first in excellence, was William Harvey,* who, both as an engraver and designer, stands pre-eminent at this day. His fellow-apprentice was William Temple (who left off wood-engraving, and commenced linen draper in Newcastle). He was a faithful copyist, and his pieces were honestly or clearly cut. The last apprentice I had was John Armstrong, who is now pursuing his business in London. I have not gone down in regular succession with my pupils; but I have noticed all those who, in my estimation, were worth notice. And, now when the time is fast approaching for my winding up all my labours, I may be allowed to name my own son and partner, whose time has been taken up with attending to all the branches of our business; and who, I trust, will not let wood-engraving go down; and, though he has not shown any partiality towards it, yet the talent is there, and I hope he will call it forth.

* [1796–1866.]